How to Take Money from Wall Street

Learn to Profit in Bull and Bear Markets

Tony Oz

GOLDMAN BROWN
BUSINESS MEDIA INC.

Published by Goldman Brown Business Media Inc.
P.O. Box 3043, Laguna Hills, CA 92654.

ISBN 0-9679435-1-5

Printed in the United States of America.

To My Wife Jodi, and My Son Jordan,

You have made my life complete.

I love you both.

Disclaimer

TABLE OF CONTENTS

SECTION I

The Holly Grail

SECTION II

How to Find Stocks to Trade

Acknowledgements

Cover: My stock trading setup. TriKinetic computer powering six LCD monitors running RealTick software. Photo taken by Anat Finck. Cover design by Russell and Julie Paris from jrp-graphics.com.

Many thanks to my wife Jodi and my son Jordan for making me smile Every day. I am sorry that I took so much time away from you while writing this book.

I want to thank Rachel, Betty, Orry, Abraham, Carissa, Daliah, and the rest of the staff at Goldman Brown Business Media Inc.

I want to thank MarrGwen and Stuart Townsend for developing RealTick, the best stock trading software in the world. Your product has enabled me to take my trading to the next level. Many thanks.

I want to thank my tech guys at TriKinetic.com for building me the dream Stock Trading Station.

Many thanks to my dear friends Steve Moebius, Kevin Britko, Alex and Andrea Maimon, Joe Yavetz, Scott Webster, Jerry Rabenberg, Garbis Laleian, William Zhu, Baron Robertson, Richard Rueb, Chris Wheeler, Michael Turner, Peggy Gudenas, Jeff Schankerman, Pete Stolcers, Cindy Cromwell, Noriko, Bruce, and my Happy-Hour friends, Michael, Keith, Steve, Mark, Brian, Beth, Meg, Gail, Henry, Courtney, Ross, Phil, Jeramie, Brenton, Kenny, Forest, Deron, Ed, Chris, Vadym, Larisa and Dave.

I feel that I owe so many professionals in the industry a debt of gratitude. I want to thank my colleagues and friends for their outstanding work in providing education for traders: Robert Deel, Ken Calhoun, Stan Kim, Dan Gibby, Gary Anderson, Mark Cook, Alan Farley, Rogan LaBier, Brandon Fredrickson, Toni Hansen, Michael Williams, Eric Patterson, Ray Grant, David Nassar, Ted Tesser, Sunny Harris, Linda Raschke, Toni Turner, the crew at 100 S. Wacker, and to all the ones I forgot, please forgive me.

Thanks to Tim Bourquin and Jim Sugarman. Thanks to all the members of the Market Technicians Association. Thanks to all the members of Daytraders USA, and special thanks to all my students. You have inspired me to write this book for you.

Special thanks to my dear friend Rick LaPoint for both the priceless contribution he has given to our industry and for developing the Tony Oz Stock Market Calculator.

Note from the Author

Hi Everyone,

Before you go on to read this book, I want to tell you a few things. First, although the title of this book is <u>How to Take Money from Wall Street</u>, I want you to know that stock trading is not a get-rich-quick scheme. On the contrary, stock trading is a business, and as you will read in this book, I take this business seriously.

Next, I want to share with you my outlook on how you can learn the most out of this book. I strongly believe that it takes time and pace to learn anything in life. That said, I am recommending that you take the time to study every chart, example, case study or table that are featured in this book. Please work out the math problems and make sure that you can clearly see and understand the references I make to every illustration in this book.

This book is not a novel and was not written for a speedy recreational read. I wrote this book with the intention of giving you both a text book and a reference book for stock trading.

I have been fortunate to work with numerous stock traders over the years, and I have paid close attention to the growing-pains they went through on their path to either success or failure. The most common mistake many of them made was information overload. Because they wanted to learn it all in a day, they bought books, tapes, attended seminars, joined message boards and chat rooms, all at the same time, in their search for the sure thing.

Here is my suggestion to you: Study this book (don't read it, study it!) Then, paper-trade the different strategies that are featured here. Give yourself at least three months to see if you can use one or more of the strategies in this book. While you are trying to incorporate what you have learned into your trading system, you must not try anything else. Don't read another book and don't take any seminars. This should increase the odds for success.

I want to thank you for both buying this book and taking the time to study it. I hope that you will be able to profit from it in the future.

Trade Smart!

CHAPTER 1

The Money Tree

If you are reading this book, then it is safe to assume that you have an interest in the stock market. I think it is also safe to assume that you *want* to make money in the stock market. You are not looking to lose money, are you? Of course, not!

What I will try to do in this book is share with you my 15 years of experience in the stock market. I will attempt to do this is in a simple conversational writing style. I want you to hear me loud and clear as if we were having a cup of coffee together. I will do so in an honest way. I will tell you what worked for me over the years, but more importantly what did not work. I will share with you stories of great profits, and I will share with you stories of great losses. I will share with you the success I enjoy, and I will share with you the most painful mistakes that I have made.

The first section of this book deals with what it takes to succeed in this business. In this section, you will learn how to put the building blocks together and develop an effective trading system. I will focus on the *Holy Grail* of stock trading - superior money management and exceptional mindset. I will walk you through not only the rules and guidelines, but also the development process and logic behind the *Holy Grail*. I will also try to provide you with a road map and guide you to the best tools you can find today.

The second section of this book deals with application. You will learn how to apply high-probability stock picking strategies to your trading system on a daily basis. You will learn how to spot great opportunities and profit from them.

One of the challenges I am facing as an author is trying to make this book easy to understand for the beginner, yet, not boring to intermediate or advanced trader. If you are a true beginner, I suggest that you first read a primer book or the beginner's crash course on www.tonyoz.com. I believe it would make following this book somewhat easier. I would also like you to know that all the stories you will read in this book are real! However, in order to protect the integrity of this publication, the names of the companies and people involved will be changed. It is important that you understand that knowing which stock I lost 30% of my money on, or which Wall Street firm caused me a huge loss is not significant. However, it is significant to know why I lost money, and what were the lessons that I learned. Are you ready? Let's get right to it!

Before we proceed to learn how to take money from Wall Street, we must understand how this mega business works. The questions that we want to answer are basically: Who makes money on Wall Street? And, how can I get a share of that pie?

When I talk about Wall Street, I am referring to the two major stock exchanges, the NYSE and Nasdaq, where shares of publicly owned companies are traded in the open market. When an individual is buying stock in one of these publicly traded companies, he becomes the proud owner of a share of that company. The reason he is buying a share in the company is simply because he thinks that he is getting value for his money, and he expects that the value of his ownership will increase over a certain time frame. When this individual buys the stock, he buys it from another person who thinks that the stock price of the company is overvalued, and he expects that the price will go down over a certain time frame. There are two sides to the transaction, a buyer, and a seller. What motivate either one of them to buy or sell the stock are their **expectations**. The overall expectations of investors will determine the driving force behind stock prices and will produce the current supply and demand for the security. But, how do investors know what to expect? Who is telling them what to expect? My friends, the one who tells investors what to expect is normally the one that makes the money. Did you ever hear the words *strong buy recommendation*? Did you ever hear the words *upgrade* or *downgrade*? You probably have. These words are directly related to some of the most painful lessons I have learned in this business.

In 1986, by way of a miracle, I got my risk capital. I won a lottery ticket, which gave me $8,000 to speculate with. I was already following the stock market on a daily basis prior to winning the lottery ticket, because most of my family members were speculators. I had great passion for stocks, but I was faced with the greatest question of them all. **How do I find the right stock?** This is the same question that will come up on a daily basis over the next 10 years, and I am sure most of you are trying to answer this same question on a daily basis as well. I was going to use simple logic to answer this question. I asked myself, who do I know that has enjoyed the greatest success in the stock market over the last year? The answer was my uncle David. "Great!" I told myself and called my uncle. When he got on the phone, I asked him for a stock tip. He told me that he does not believe in giving out tips, but he will make an exception for me. He told me to buy XYZ stock, and I did. What a great tip it was. I sold my stock four weeks later for 180% gain! Wow, this is easy, I thought to myself. After I sold the stock, my uncle told me that I made a mistake. I couldn't see how making 180% in four weeks was a mistake, but I didn't say anything. My uncle refused to give me another stock tip and encouraged me to do my own research.

Over the next three months, XYZ stock went up 500%. It was extremely painful to watch it during that time. The pain was even more severe, because I was consistently losing money trying to pick stocks on my own over the same time period. My stock picking method was to simply buy stocks that had good news. I did not know that when the news came out, it was time to sell and take profits. So, what I did was provide liquidity to those who were holding the stock in anticipation of the good news and were selling the stock to realize profits. After making the same mistake more than a handful of times, I realized that I was buying the absolute high. **The market tends to overreact to major news events, good or bad**. This was the first big lesson I learned. I realized that if I had done the exact opposite of what I had been doing, I would have made money, so I decided to do the exact opposite from that point on. The only problem was that I was restricted from selling short, so the only way for me to play was to buy stocks, which had really bad news and suffered significant price drop as a result. I did quite well using this method for a while. However, I could only make very short-term trades on these stocks, because who wants to own a stock that does not seem to have a very bright future?

I enjoyed a good run for a while, and I was scanning the newspapers on a daily basis searching for disaster news. In 1989, XYZ Company issued a news release saying that they have to restate earnings, because of accounting irregularities. The stock price was cut in half the following day, and I bought it at 7.25. The stock did not bounce at all and kept going down. At the end of the trading day, it was at 4.50. I decided to double my position. The stock kept going lower over the next week, and it was now trading at 2.75. The stock came down in price from an all time high of 85. "It can't go any lower," I told myself and doubled my position again. My average cost was 4.32. I kept thinking that it had to bounce. Well, it didn't. In fact, the stock was halted a few days later, and never opened for trading again. I lost the entire money I had in the position. I lost 36% of my account on this one trade! That was my first BIG money management lesson. It was a complex lesson in the sense that it had very important implications.

First, **I must limit the maximum loss I will take on one position**. Next, **I will not add to a losing position**. Finally, **I will not have a concentrated position in one stock**.

It wasn't until 1991 that I came across Technical Analysis. I remember my first attempt to make sense out of a chart. To be honest, charts did not make any sense to me. It looked to me like drawings of girls in ponytails rather than anything that suggested future price movement or market psychology. It just simply did not register in my head, so I gave up on it very quickly and resumed my news related trading style (also known as momentum trading). In

3

late 1993, I finally had enough confidence, ignoring the warnings from those who cared about me, to open a margin account. It wasn't that I was seeking the extra leverage as much as I wanted to be able to play both sides of the market. I wanted to be able to profit from falling stock prices. However, like most investors, I was not comfortable with the idea of selling short. I though it was "un-American" to do so. How can I cheer for a stock to go down in price when all the people who own it will lose money?

I finally got over it, and when one of the leading computer makers reported better than expected loss (they didn't lose as much money as the street was anticipating), I executed my first short sale. Prior to the news, the stock has gone up from 25 to 28.75. I called my broker and told him to sell the stock short at the open. The stock opened at 32.75 and I covered my short at 28.75 about 30 minutes later.

This was one of the biggest percentage gains I have experienced in such a short time frame. This taught me a very important lesson. **I must master trading both sides of the market**. I would say that in the six months following the big win I had on my first ever short sale, at least 40% of my trades were on the short side of the market.

1994 was a pivot year for me. I got married and moved in to my wife's place. She lived just five minutes away from where the *Investor's Business Daily*, *The Daily Graphs,* and other William O'Neil publications were printed. I started going there on a daily basis and learned technical analysis from the pros. I remember walking into their office with my *QuoTreck* in one hand and my car phone in the other. I would spend hours going over the huge database of charts, on a daily basis.

While at the office, I met many retired brokers who were now making a living as investors. They were giving me many educational tips, but no stock tips. I was envious of their experience, and I yearned to learn. I knew how important it was to try to learn as much as I possibly could from these pros. I finally got my prayers answered when one of them agreed to teach me technical analysis. I paid him $5,000 to spend two weeks with me and teach me how to take money from the stock market. He had one condition prior to agreeing to teach me, and that was that I could not execute even a single trade during the two weeks. I have to admit that the two weeks I spent with my tutor were crucial to my future success, and the $5,000 I spent was probably the best investment I have ever made. I learned another valuable lesson. **I must invest in my education**.

I was now armed with a dangerous weapon. I have added chart-reading tech-

4

niques to my stock-trading arsenal. I started to modify my trading system just in time for the great bull market that was going to start soon. I still made some momentum plays, but I was now looking to master swing trading. I wanted to profit from a two to ten day move on a stock. I was looking to potentially hold more than one open position and manage my open positions with strict rules.

As I was building my very own trading system, I was still faced with the same problem. Although I knew how to read charts and recognize high-probability opportunities, I still did not know where to find my candidates. What I mean is that if you put a chart in front of my eyes, I could recognize an opportunity if it was there, but how could I get the best charts in front of my eyes in those stone-age days? That was the biggest challenge. This is where the *Investors' Business Daily* came in handy. Since I lived so close to their offices, I would get the paper approximately six hours after the market closed. That gave me all night to get ready for the next day. What I liked most about the paper was that it had tables, which featured stocks that were moving in price on higher than average volume. While I was learning how to read charts, I also learned how important it is to measure the intensity of a particular pattern. **Volume as an indicator measures the intensity of a price move**. Consequently, the tables in the newspaper presented me with a list of candidates for potential trades.

Life was great! My returns were consistently improving, and I was getting very good at forecasting short-term price movements. However, I didn't quite master the mindset it takes to be truly happy. In fact, I was suffering from the hindsight syndrome so many traders experience in their career. I was simply seeing the glass half empty rather than half full. For instance, I would buy a stock at 26 and sell it at 29 pocketing a profit of three points. Shortly after, I would see the same stock I sold at 29 trading at 35. It was the money that I left on the table that started to get the best of me. I was not happy with the three points profit anymore. In fact, I was upset about the 6 points I left behind. Was I getting greedy? You better believe it!

It was time for me to sit down and figure out how to maximize my profits, and I did just that. I sat down and started to write out a new business plan for my trading system. I was experienced enough by then to realize that I needed to explore new ways to increase my overall returns, and I found the perfect solution. Since most of the stocks I was trading were "high quality" stocks, I noticed that these stocks always found a way to move higher over a longer time frame. "Aha," I told myself, and decided that from this point forward, a portion of my capital will be used for position trading with time frames of three months or longer. This was my 1995 new-year resolution. However, if I was to start position trading, potentially holding stocks over a longer time frame, I felt it was important to complete the circle and master fundamental analysis. I had already read William O'Neil's book that teaches the CANSLIM method of investing and understood that **year-over-year earnings growth is the most important element for sustainable stock price appreciation**.

The crystal ball dropped in Time Square and we all welcomed the new-year. 1994 was my best year in the market so far, and I was looking to do even better in 1995. As most of you who have been following the market know, 1995 was probably one of the greatest years for the bulls. It was almost impossible not to make money if you owned any stock. Unless, of course, you made the same mistakes that I made.

It was March of 1995, and I had created a portfolio of eight stocks. I had all my cash in these promising companies, and was using margin for short-term trading. I came across a listed stock in the communications sector that enjoyed great interest from investors. The stock had traded up from two to ten in about two months. I bought this stock at seven, and it made up 15% of my portfolio. As I was following the stock price action on my quote machine one day in March, I noticed that the stock was exploding higher. It was up almost two points and trading at 11.87 on five times its daily average volume. It was an hour before the close, and I decided to make a day trade on the stock.

I called my broker and placed a buy order using my margin buying power. I got a fill at 11.87. In a matter of 20 minutes, the stock went up to 12.87, and I called my broker. It was 40 minutes to the close, and I wished to sell my position and take my profits. When the broker asked me what I wanted to do, I told him to sell the stock at the market. "Mr. Oz, the computer is not taking my order," he said. "What do mean? Sell it! Sell it! Sell it!" I screamed as loud as I could. He seemed very confused, because the order kept giving him an error. "I'll be right back," he said. I was waiting on hold for 20 minutes before he returned.

"The stock is halted, news pending," he told me when he came back. To be honest, I never thought a stock could get halted in the middle of the trading day. I never saw it happened before, but it can surely happen, and I was about to learn an extremely painful lesson. When I entered the trade, I did not plan on holding the stock overnight. I thought I was managing risk properly, but I was very wrong! The stock did not open for trading the following two days. When it finally opened, it was trading at 5!

I lost 37% of my account on this one stock. How is that for risk management? There is no need to answer this question. I was furious with my misfortune on this trade. I felt that I was robbed of my hard earned money. I was so mad that I completely ignored everything I had learned so far in the stock market, and I didn't care to learn the lesson of this last trade. **When managing risk, one must think of the absolute worst-case scenario**. In this case, it was that any stock can be halted during the trading day and receive a 61% haircut once it opens for trading again.

Following this horrifying experience, I found myself in the poorest mindset I have ever had as a trader. I could only think about one thing. I wanted to get even with the market! I was looking for a stock that could double over the next year. I was going to use 100% margin to buy this stock, and in 12 months bring my account 40% higher than it was prior to the disaster trade. I was desperate, and I got my golden opportunity.

XYZ Technology was a company that manufactured semiconductors products. It was trading at 90 when one of the biggest Wall Street firms issued a strong buy and a 12-month price target north of 200. I decided that this stock was my lottery ticket, and I went all out and bought it at 94.50. I used 100% margin, and I was now holding eight stocks in my portfolio. XYZ Technology made up 62% of my equity and 31% of my total portfolio. The other seven stocks I held made up 138% (using margin) of my equity and 69% of my portfolio. My position in XYZ Technology was very concentrated. In fact, it was about three times the size of any other single stock I had in my portfolio, but it was a sure winner, so I wasn't worried.

XYZ Technology hit a high of 94.75 the day I bought it and started falling down like a rock. It was trading at 72, and I was forced to sell a part of my position to avoid a margin call. However, there was no way I was going to sell my sure-thing, not after the analysts said it was going to be over 200 in twelve months. So, I did what all amateurs do. I studied my portfolio carefully and picked my best performing stock and sold it. I then bought a little bit more of XYZ Technology. It was a bargain to buy a $200 bill for $72, don't you think?

Some more time went by and XYZ Technology went down to 60. Again, I was forced to sell a part of my portfolio to avoid a margin call. I'm sure you guessed it by now, I picked my second best performing stock and sold it. To make a long story short, I kept selling all my other stocks while XYZ Technology kept going down in price. When XYZ Technology was trading at 45, I had no other stocks left in my portfolio. XYZ Technology made up 100% of my holdings, and my account was down another 50%.

XYZ Technology kept going down and when it hit 41, I couldn't take the pain anymore and sold it. My account equity now was 28% of what it used to be prior to the disaster of the halted stock. After I sold XYZ Technology, the stock went down to 16. I would have lost all my money had I not thrown in the towel. Do you want to know how costly this trade was? The seven stocks that I had in my portfolio prior to entering XYZ Technology went up 380% on average over the next 12 months. I learned another valuable lesson. **Sell your losers and hang on to the winners!** In fact, four years later, that same portfolio of seven stocks would have been worth well over 20 million dollars.

This XYZ Technology trade also taught me a lesson about the Wall Street moneymaking machine. The firm that gave the stock the upgrade was unloading its huge position in the stock. In fact, a class-action lawsuit was filed against them for their unethical practice. This taught me another important lesson. **Don't buy a stock or hang on to a stock because some analyst says it is a great buy.** In many cases, analysts will upgrade stocks, so their firm can sell out their inventory in these stocks. I learned this lesson in a very painful way.

Once I sold my position in XYZ Technology, I decided to take a break from the market. I needed to give my wounds time to heal. I was determined to learn from all my mistakes and put together a trading system that will stand the test of time. I needed rules and guidelines that would help me maximize returns from my strength, and at the same time, protect me from my weakness. I had to spend a lot of time inside my head in order to do so. It took me six months to put it all together, and it was well worth every minute of it. Once I felt confidant in my trading system, I started trading again, and I haven't looked back since.

CHAPTER 2

I Am Sorry, But You Can't Take My Money

"There is nothing like losing all you have in the world for teaching you what not to do. And when you know what not to do in order not to lose money, you begin to learn what to do in order to win. Did you get that? You begin to learn!" ~ *Reminiscences of a Stock Operator* by Edwin Lefevre.

I didn't quite lose all that I had in the world, but it certainly felt that way. I knew that I needed to construct a solid money management system that would protect my capital, yet, help me maximize profits as well. The following is my money management rules and guidelines, which I believe are the first step to successful trading. I am going to walk you through the different events that helped me develop my money management system. I will do so, because I think it is extremely important that you see the major events and costly lessons it took to develop the final product. I am sure many of you will relate to some of the pain and the different stages it took to develop my system, and it is my hope, that I can save many of you the pain it takes to develop a winning money management system.

Up to this point, I had been in the market for almost nine years, and I had learned that it is important to distinguish between investing and trading strategies. These two forms of market participation have different time frames, and in order not to mix the two together, I realized that I should have separate accounts for investments and for short-term trading.

The reason I came to the conclusion that I must separate my accounts was a trade I made on an HMO stock (XYZ) in 1995. I bought the stock at 60.25. The stock had strong support at 60. My price target was 65, which was the resistance level. If XYZ was to trade back up to 64.75, I was going to sell the stock. Prior to entering the trade, I knew that if XYZ traded lower than 60, I must exit the trade. Can you guess what happened next? XYZ traded down to 59.25. It broke through support, but I didn't sell it. Do you know why I didn't sell it? I'll tell you. I did not sell it, because I liked it long-term. It was a great company, and it had a promising future…

Two weeks went by, and XYZ was trading at 53. I was down over seven points on my position. I was starting to feel the pain, but I told myself, "it will come back, XYZ is a great company." To make a long story short, XYZ kept going down, and I finally could not take the pain anymore and sold it at 49.37. I lost almost 11 points on the trade.

The lesson I learned from this trade was that I was not objective. I let myself change the time frame after the trade went against me, and that is one of the biggest mistakes you can make as a short-term trader. This HMO Company was trading on the Nasdaq at the time. It later moved to the New York Stock Exchange and was trading in single digits. I could have lost a fortune on this position.

After enduring some serious pain on XYZ Technology and seeing the HMO stock trading in single digits, I decided that I was going to learn my lesson once and for all. I took a sheet of paper and wrote in big letters, "**Dear Wall Street, I am sorry, but you can't take my money.**" I decided to make capital preservation my number one goal.

In order to achieve my number one goal, I had to become very familiar with both general market risk and the risks of individual trades. I then needed to build a shield that would protect me from my biggest weakness. I needed to protect myself from Greed.

However, before I could build the sought after protective shield, I had to start thinking of stock trading as a business rather than a hobby. Trading stocks for a living is a business and it requires more work than speculators realize. Stock trading, just like any other start-up business, is vulnerable to the same three elements that make any other business fail.

1. The absence of a solid business plan
2. Lack of capital
3. Weak management

A solid business plan is our trading system, which needs to be developed prior to making the first trade. A business plan in stock trading is what many refer to as a trading system. A trading system, simply stated, is a set of rules and goals, which a trader has developed over time, that are followed religiously. A good business plan will be comparable to a tried and tested trading system.

Any business plan, or a trading system, should include all of the resources you are willing to commit in pursuing the goals of your business. Since the goal of every business is simply to make as much money as possible, your business plan should answer the questions: "How am I going to make money in the stock market, consistently?" And more importantly, "How can I lose the least amount of money while I am learning this business?"

Next, capital is needed to make the trading system work. If we compare stock trading to a retail store, capital can be compared to inventory. If you have no inventory to sell, you can't possibly make money in the retail business. Capital is an essential element for launching any business, and it is important to determine how much capital is needed upfront in order to give a business a good chance to succeed. The essence of capital in stock trading is equal to the essence of oxygen to a living organism. In the absence of oxygen, a living organism will die. Without sufficient capital, a business will fail.

I wrote the first rule in my trading system, *"**My number one goal is to protect my capital under all circumstances.**"* I knew from past experience that stock traders who were not well capitalized would normally take bigger risks, and if the rewards were not there in a short period of time, the high-risk plays would bankrupt the trader. This means that as a professional stock trader, I should not take extreme risks attempting to hit a home run on every trade. A stock trader who wishes to make his million in one day will be hung in one week.

For those of you who are considering this business, whether you make it or fail at it, it is only worth a shot if you can sustain the loss of your risk capital and the time you have committed. Obviously, one has to be financially comfortable in order to be able to commit risk capital and also have the time for this new business venture. If you do not have the luxury of doing so, then you will be playing against bigger odds.

Even if you have the best trading system available today and a lot of money to trade with, you could still lose it all if you do not have the mindset and discipline to manage your trading system. Strong management in stock trading is the ability to follow and execute the rules and guidelines of your business plan. In other words, the business plan is the bible of trading, and strict management is the mindset and discipline that it takes to follow the laws of this bible. The mindset and discipline are what ties the knots together and turns a promising trading system into a profitable one.

When I studied some of my worst trades in greater detail, I found out that I lost a lot more money on these trades than I would have potentially earned from them had I been right. My risk was greater than my potential reward. This was unacceptable risk management methodology, and it was time to change it. The plan I came up with was very simple. First, every potential trade must have a plan. This plan must include Entry Price, Target Price, Stop Loss Price, and Time Frame. Next, every trade must present me with greater reward than the risk I would be taking on that trade. I decided that I would only enter trades that presented me with an opportunity to make three times the amount of money I was willing to risk, which means that the reward must be three times greater than the risk.

After further analysis, I realized that I could have gone bankrupt many times in the early stages of my career had the worst happened, because of the big bets I was making when I was hot for a stock or for the market. Luckily, I did not lose it all, but I figured out that my **short-term trading account should never have more money in it than the total amount of money I could afford to lose!** After I wrote down this golden rule, I made my first move and opened an account that was going to be used only for short-term trading, and funded it with risk capital that I could afford to lose.

I decided that I was going to use margin in my short-term account and cash only in my investment accounts. Consequently, the amount of money I used to fund my short-term account was half the amount of money I could afford to lose, because when you trade on margin, you can lose more than the principle amount.

Once I knew the total amount of money I could afford to lose, I needed to set up a rule for the maximum amount of money I can lose on one position. My initial money management system was very simple, yet it was very aggressive. I set up a rule for the maximum loss on one position to be at 1.5% of equity. I also set up a rule for diversity. I must not take a position in one stock that is greater than 25% of equity (12.5% of buying power).

Based on these rules, if I wanted to buy XYZ stock at 50, and I had $100,000 in my account, how many shares could I buy?

25% of $100,000 = $25,000 (maximum amount of money for one position)
$25,000 / 50 (stock price) = 500 shares

How low can I let it go before I have to sell it?

I cannot lose more than 1.5% of my equity on one trade.
1.5% of $100,000 = $1,500 Maximum Dollar Loss (MDL)
1500 (MDL) / 500 (number of shares) = 3
50 (purchase price) − 3 (Maximum Point Loss) = 47

If XYZ goes below 47, I must sell it!

From that point on, I followed this money management system religiously. Every month, I studied my trading records to see how I was doing. I was using different ways to measure my performance. I first started with a simple win/loss ratio, which only shows the percentage of time I was right versus the percentage of time I was wrong. However, this did not give me any kind of performance number that was relative to the risks I was taking and the rewards

I was reaping. For instance, I could be right 80% of the time and still lose money. This is when I figured out that I had to study things differently. I decided to concentrate on the risks and rewards of my system, so I added all the losses I had in one month and divided that number by the total number of losing trades. This gave me the average loss per losing trade. I then added all the winners I had in one month and divided that number by the total number of winning trades. This gave me the average profit I made on a winning trade.

I was having a lot of fun analyzing these numbers not only because I always found math fascinating, but also because I truly believed that I could learn many valuable lessons. I was obsessed to get a return figure that would be directly related to the risk I was taking. Then, it hit me. Reward to risk ratio equals:

(Profit / All Profitable Trades) / (Losses / All Losing Trades)

Using the above formula, if I made a profit of 10,000 on 25 profitable trades, and I lost 7,000 on 35 losing trades, then (10,000 / 25) / (7000 / 35) = 2. My reward to risk equals two. Therefore, for every dollar I risk in the market, I will make two dollars back. I used this formula for a while before I realized that I was doing something wrong. My risk number was only covering the losing trades, but not the winning trades. I also generalized all my trades into one group rather than sorting all my trades by the type of strategy I was trading. It was time to fix this mistake.

The following month, I sorted all my trading records by the strategies I was using and the source of the trade (how I found the trade). I then fine-tuned my reward to risk formula. First, I needed to find out the average MDL (Maximum Dollar Loss) per trade. This is done by adding all the Maximum Dollar Loss (MDL) for all executed traded and dividing it by the total number of trades. Next, I needed to find out the average loss or gain I had for the month for that particular strategy. This is simply done by taking the total dollar return and dividing it by the total number of trades. Once I figured out this formula, I was able to analyze my records in more depth and figure out the true reward for my risk.

[(Total Profits - Total Loss) / # of trades)] / Average MDL = Reward to Risk Ratio

Suppose that last month, I made a profit of 10,000 on 7 trades, and I lost 4,000 on 15 trades on stocks that showed up on my Usual Suspects Scan. Let's say that the average MDL for the 22 trades I executed was 265. Using the above formula, what is my reward to risk ratio for the Usual Suspects Strategy?

$$[(10,000 - 4000) / 22] / 265 = 1.03$$

This tells me that for every dollar I risked, I made $1.03 in profit. This number is extremely valuable, and it plays a major role in my overall risk management system. I will show you how I use this number to determine risk in the chapter *Defense Wins Championships*.

After my loss on XYZ Technology, I realized that I needed to protect myself from another weakness I had. Since I was doing very well up to that point, it was all just numbers to me. It was almost like a video game that I was just scoring points, and I wanted to break my own record and reach a higher total score for the game. The point I am trying to make is that I forgot there was real money on the line. But once I took the big loss on XYZ Technology, the loss was so severe that now it was talking to me in dollars and cents. Let me try to illustrate what I mean.

Let's say you open an account with $10,000. You begin trading, and you execute 35 trades and make 80% on your money in one month. The next month you execute 32 trades and make 120%. The following month you execute 37 trades and make 80%. Then, you lose 30% of your money on one trade. Do you have any idea how much you have just lost on your one trade? You just lost more than twice the amount of capital you opened your account with. You just lost over twenty thousand dollars! More often than not, it would be psychologically devastating.

Because I wanted to avoid this from happening at all cost, I decided that I would sweep all the profits out of my account on a weekly basis. At the end of each week, I call my broker and order a check! I keep my short-term trading account at a fixed principle amount. Everything over that amount is swept out of the account. If I made $100 or $10,000 that week, it does not matter; I will order a check for that amount. I use that money to pay my bills, take my wife out to dinner, travel, or buy Jordan new shoes. If I have made more money than I planned on spending, I will allocate it to longer-term investments. This system allows me to enjoy the fruits of my work and invest for long-term growth. If I have a losing week, I do not add money back into the account. I will work with the same capital until I get back the fixed principle amount and draw checks again. This will prevent me from losing a lot if I hit a slump.

Like most percentage-based money management systems, my system had a HUGE flaw in it. In 1998, volatility started to increase dramatically, and stocks had larger intraday trading-ranges. This represented a major challenge to my money management system.

In April of 1998, I sold short 600 shares of XYZ stock at 49.93. I had a 2.5 points stop loss in place (1.5% of equity), so if XYZ was to trade higher than 52.43, I was going to cover my short and close the position. Shortly after I entered the position, XYZ stock went straight up, and my stop was triggered. However, by the time my order to buy XYZ at the market was executed, XYZ was trading at 64. The stock went straight up like a moon rocket. I lost 14.07 X 600 = 8,442 = 8.44% of my equity. This loss was 5.62 times greater than what I could afford to lose on this trade according to my trading system. Consequently, I learned another important lesson. I needed to make an adjustment to my money management system. I needed to modify the money management rules and guidelines for the different strategies I use.

Since most of my trading strategies are based on technical setups, I think that I must cover technical analysis at this point.

CHAPTER 3

Technical Analysis

"So, again, we come to the question of whether Sentiment creates the Chart, or the Chart leads the Market. Ultimately, the charts are created by Sentiment, which is based on two things: Earnings, both Actual -- and probably more important -- Anticipated, and the Anticipation of Trend." ~ Rick LaPoint

I think that charts give us the true picture of supply and demand for a stock over a certain period of time. The price action, which is captured in a chart format, paints the picture of investors' expectations and the overall sentiment and psychology of the market. Charts also show us the changes in investors' expectations, sentiment and psychology, which translates into changes in supply and demand for a particular stock. I have studied the different patterns of investors' expectations through technical analysis, and I have concluded that price charts are essential for both short-term traders and investors.

I will be using both Bar Charts and Candlestick Charts to illustrate my strategies in this book.

Bar Charts

Each bar shows four different price fields for any given day. These price fields include the **opening** price of the day, the **high** price of the day, the **low** price of the day, and the **closing** price of the day.

Opening Price – This is the execution price of the first trade of the day.
High – This is the highest price point that the stock traded at that day.
Low – This is the lowest price the stock traded at that day.
Closing Price – This is the price of the last trade of the day.

Candlestick Charts

Candlestick charts record the same data; however, it is somewhat easier to see the range between the opening price and the closing price for the time period the candlestick covers. Here are the differences between a white candle and a black candle.

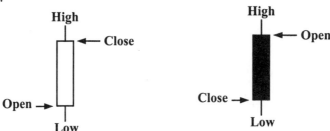

A white candle means that the closing price was higher than the opening price. A black candle means that closing price was lower than the opening price.

There are many chart patterns and technical indicators that are used by professionals on Wall Street who try to forecast future price movement. You can absolutely drive yourself crazy trying to study all the different patterns and indicators available today. In fact, I did so myself, and after spending thousands of hours trying to learn all I could about the art of chart reading, I came to the conclusion that to be advanced in technical analysis I must keep things simple. Most indicators are derived from price or volume data, and in most cases the signals they generate actually lag the obvious picture that is painted by the price bars. After I realized that, I started to focus on what the price bars were trying to tell me. I learned to spot what was truly important in the charts - the trend, major and secondary support levels, major and secondary resistance levels, and volume.

When we use technical analysis to try and forecast future price changes for a stock, we must first determine the overall direction the stock is moving in. This is known as the **trend** of the stock. This is the simplest, yet most important element in chart reading. This should be the first thing to jump at you when you look at a price chart of a stock. There are 3 trends that should be easy to identify:

- An uptrend - Where the price of a stock is trending (moving) higher over the studied period of time featured in the chart.
- A downtrend - Where the price of a stock is trending lower over the studied period of time featured in the chart.
- No trend - Where a stock is moving sideways over the studied period of time featured in the chart.

Support and Resistance

Once I identify the trend, I look for the major price levels of support and resistance. The mechanism of price movement in a stock is attributed to supply and demand. The total number of shares offered for sale versus the total number of shares desired by buyers at a given price, will determine if the price will go up or down. The fluctuations in the price of a stock are directly related to these factors and can be seen on a chart. The simplest way to look at it is by analyzing a one-day price movement for a stock. The following example illustrates a typical trading day for XYZ stock.

XYZ opens for trading at 73.50. During the morning, there were more sellers than buyers and the stock went down to 71.50. This was the lowest price of the day that XYZ traded. At this point, more buyers were interested in purchasing the stock, because the price was very attractive to them, so the quantity in demand was greater than the quantity in supply. Consequently, XYZ shares started to trade higher and at 1:30 PM it was trading at 74.50. This was the highest price that XYZ traded. The scales change again and quantity supplied was greater than quantity demanded, and sellers pushed the price of XYZ down to 74.10 where it closed the trading session. Let's chart this data and analyze it further.

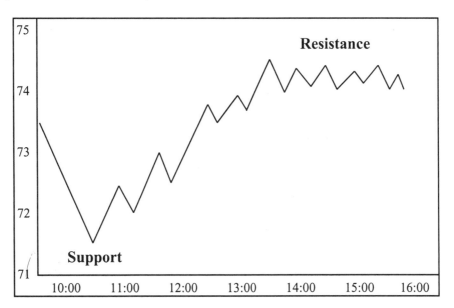

As you can see, XYZ traded down from 73.50 to 71.50 where it found a bottom (support), then traded back up to 74.50 where it topped out (resistance). The question is, why? Why didn't XYZ go lower than 71.50? Why didn't it go higher than 74.50? The answer, of course, is found in the laws of supply and demand.

19

The laws of supply and demand for any product or service are very simple.

1. If quantity demanded is greater than quantity in supply, prices will go up.
2. If quantity in supply is greater than quantity in demand, prices will go down.

The reason XYZ share price did not go higher than 74.50 is simply because, at that point, the quantity in supply was greater than the quantity in demand.

The next question is, why was the quantity demanded higher than the quantity supplied at 71.50, and why was the quantity in supply greater than the quantity in demand at 74.50? In other words, what determines supply and demand in the stock market?

The reason there was more quantity in demand at 71.50 is simply because investors' expectations were for the stock to go up in price. The reason there was more quantity in supply at 74.50 was because investors' expectations were for the stock to go down in price. **Supply and demand in the stock market is determined by investors' expectations**.

This is how we can use this data on the following trading day: If XYZ traded back down to 71.50, we should expect buyers to step in and buy the stock. If XYZ trades back up to 74.50, we should expect selling pressure. I will be a buyer at 71.50 –71.75, and I will be a seller at 74.25 – 74.50. This easy to understand concept is the foundation of my trading system, and almost every setup I trade is based on entering a stock at a price that presents me with the greatest potential rewards and the lowest potential risk.

The following day, XYZ stock opened at 74 and traded down to 71.60 as seen on the following chart.

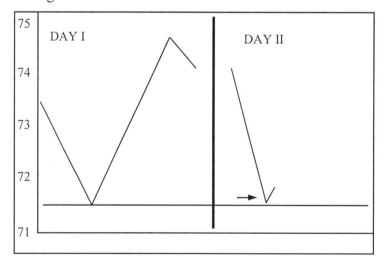

Based on the fact that 71.50 was good support for the stock, I could buy the stock at 71.64. My price target would be the resistance level at 74.50. Once I am in the trade, I must manage my position in a professional way. I know that at 71.50 the quantity demanded is greater than the quantity supplied because the majority of investors feel that the stock will move higher in price. However, investors' psychology changes rapidly with time. This change in expectations will change the overall demand. Consequently, major support and resistance levels will be penetrated, and a buy or a sell signal will be triggered.

Here is what happened next. XYZ traded up to 72.39 from the low it made at 71.60. However, the stock was facing strong selling pressure and traded down to 71.25. It penetrated through the 71.50 support level on increasing volume. The following chart shows the price action.

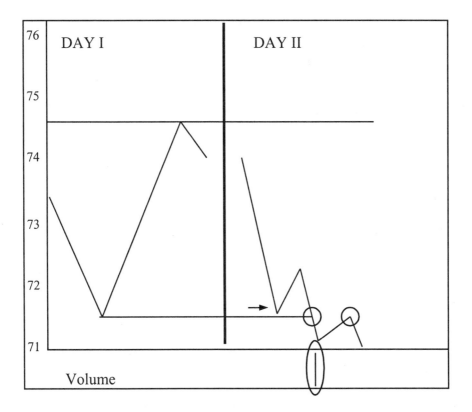

As you can see, XYZ penetrated through the support line on increasing volume. This suggests that investors' expectations had changed. Since I bought this stock because I thought that investors were going to support it again at 71.50, I must exit the trade at once. Although this is easier said than done, I must remember why I entered the trade and what I was expecting to happen. Since what I expected to happen did not happen, I must take a small loss and get out of the trade.

21

This example illustrates another law of technical analysis. If support is penetrated **successfully**, it will become resistance should the stock trade back up to the penetration level. The key word here is successfully. What we look for is an increase in volume at the penetration point. The logic is that the tables have turned around as more sellers stepped in and took the support level out. If the stock price were to go back up to that point, then interest from sellers should still be there. The increasing volume suggests that we have washed out all the investors who thought XYZ was a bargain at 71.50. As you can see in the chart, XYZ tried to rally after it penetrated the support level, but once it got close to 71.50 (the second circle on the chart), sellers took over again, and the stock kept going lower. As traders, we will try to short that rally, as I will show you later in this book.

I think it is also important to study the opposite scenario. Let's say that XYZ opened at 74 on DAY II and traded up to 74.42 as seen on the following chart.

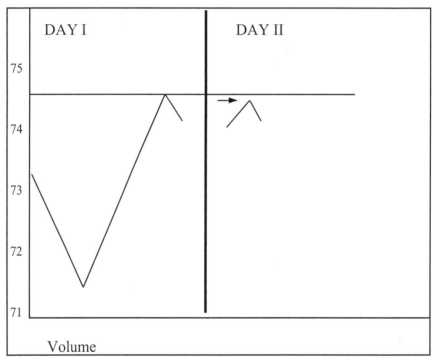

Based on the fact that 74.50 is strong resistance for the stock, I could sell XYZ short at 74.40. My price target would be the support level at 71.50. Once I am in the trade, I must manage my position in a professional way. I know that at 74.50 the quantity in supply is greater than the quantity demanded because the majority of investors feel that the stock will move lower in price. However, investors' psychology changes rapidly with time. This change in expectations will change the overall demand. Consequently, as we saw in the previous example, support and resistance levels can be penetrated.

Here is what happened next. XYZ traded down to 74.10 from the high it made at 74.42. However, the stock was facing strong buying pressure and traded up to 75.22. It penetrated through the 74.50 resistance level on increasing volume. The following chart shows the price action.

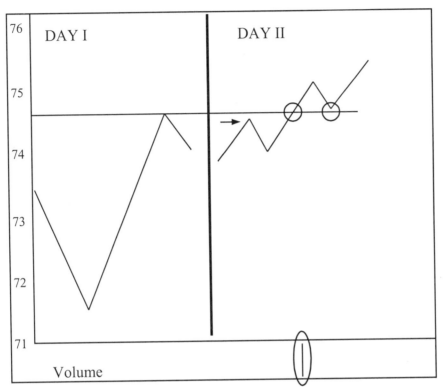

As you can see, XYZ penetrated through the resistance line on increasing volume. This suggests that investors' expectations have changed. Since I sold this stock short because I thought that investors were going to sell the stock at 74.50, I must exit the trade at once.

This example illustrates another law of technical analysis. If resistance is penetrated **successfully**, it will become support should the stock trade back down to the penetration level. The key word here is successfully. What we look for is an increase in volume at the penetration point. The logic is that the tables have turned around as more buyers stepped in and took the resistance level out. If the stock price were to go back down to that point, then interest from buyers should still be there. The increasing volume suggests that we have washed out all the investors who thought XYZ was overvalued at 74.50. As you can see in the chart, XYZ pulled back in price after it penetrated the resistance level, but once it got close to 74.50 (the second circle on the chart), buyers took over again, and the stock kept going higher. As traders, we will try to buy that pullback, as I will show you later in this book.

The absolute low price and absolute high price are the major support and resistance levels. However, there are also secondary support and resistance levels that are just as important. Those levels are found at intermediate tops and bottoms, price consolidation areas, trend-lines, moving averages and Bollinger Bands. The next section will cover the basics of secondary support and resistance levels.

Trend-Lines

A trend-line is a straight line drawn below the bottoms in a stock that is rising in prices, or over the tops in a stock that is declining in prices. **In an up-trending stock, the trend-line is another support point** to be considered. **In a down-trending stock, the trend-line is another resistance point** to consider. In an up-trending stock, we will look to buy the stock if it hits its trend-line. In a down-trending stock, we will look to sell the stock short if it hits its trend-line. Let's look at the following charts.

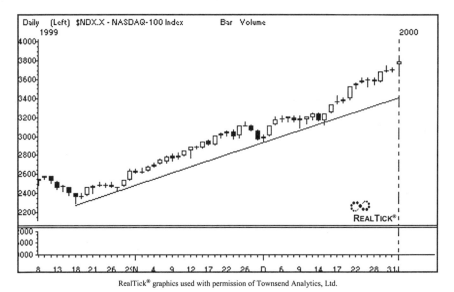

RealTick® graphics used with permission of Townsend Analytics, Ltd.

The above chart illustrates how the trend-line was supporting the price of the NASDAQ-100 Index at the end of 1999.

24

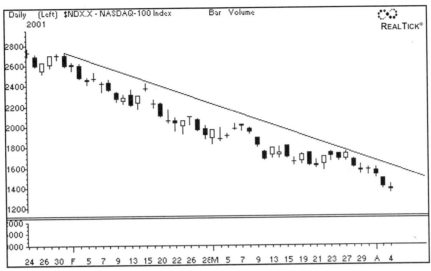

The above chart illustrates how the trend-line was another resistance level for the NASDAQ-100 Index in the first quarter of 2001.

Moving Averages

A moving average is calculated by adding together the stock prices over a certain period of time and dividing it by the total number of days. For example, if we wanted to know the average price a stock was trading over the last five days, we would add the prices of the five days and divide the number by five. For example, if XYZ closed at 56 on Monday, 58 on Tuesday, 59 on Wednesday, 58 on Thursday and 61 on Friday. The average closing price for the five days will be calculated as so: $(56+58+59+58+61)/5=58.4$

You do not have to worry about calculating the average prices yourself, because charting programs such as RealTick® will do it for you. The important thing is to understand what that number stands for.

Moving averages show the direction a stock is moving. The two most significant moving averages (MA) I use in my trading are the 50-day MA (10-week MA) and 200-day MA (40-week MA.) I also use a 10-day MA and a 20-day MA for short term trading. This is the philosophy behind the 50-day MA and 200-day MA:

If a stock is in an overall uptrend and has pulled back in price to one of these two moving averages, investors and fund managers will look at it as a golden opportunity to buy the stock. The reason behind this thinking is that if investors were willing to buy this stock at this price over the last 50 or 200 days, then it is at a bargain price.

If a stock is in an overall down-trend and has traded up in price to one of these two moving averages, investors and fund managers will look at it as a golden opportunity to get out of the stock. The reason behind this thinking is that if investors were willing to sell this stock at this price over the last 50 or 200 days, then it at an excellent price to get out of the position.

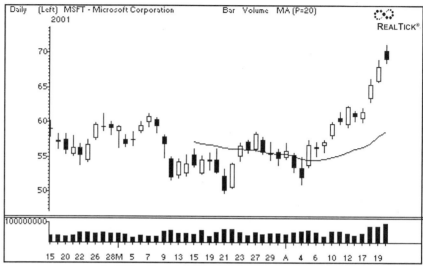

RealTick® graphics used with permission of Townsend Analytics, Ltd.

I have added a 20-day simple moving average to Microsoft's chart. The moving average appears as a line on the chart and indicates what the average price over the last 20 trading days was for Microsoft. You might have noticed that the moving average line is not present for the first 19 price bars on the chart (on the left side.) The reason is that we need to have 20 days of price data before we can have a value for an average price over the last 20 days.

MA Crossovers: In general, when a shorter term MA crosses over a longer term MA to the upside, and both slopes go up, it is a bullish signal (the value of the shorter MA is greater than the longer MA). When a longer term MA crosses over a shorter term MA to the upside, and both slopes go down, it is a bearish signal (the value of the long term MA is greater than the value of the short term MA).

I know that many traders like to use different time period MA crossovers as a part of their trading system. I have not found them to be very reliable myself, and in many cases, they were nothing more than a lagging signal stating the obvious chart pattern.

There are also weighted and exponential moving averages that can be used in trading. These are normally used to give a faster signal for a crossover. It is my belief that just like a simple moving average, both weighted and exponential moving averages also lag to signal the obvious pattern. I think it is also important that I mention that I found the simple moving averages to be more reliable support and resistance levels than weighted or exponential moving averages.

Channels and Bollinger-Bands

When a stock trades in a pattern in which drawing straight lines under the bottoms and over the tops result in two parallel lines, the area in between the lines is called a channel. We draw three parallel lines, the first over the bottoms, the second over the tops and the third at the midpoint between the two lines. This line shows us more clearly in which range of the channel the stock is currently trading. There are three types of channel trading: Horizontal Trading Channel, Declining Channel and Rising Channel. In all three cases, we buy when a stock hits the bottom range of the channel and we sell when the stock hits the top range of the channel.

Horizontal Trading Channel

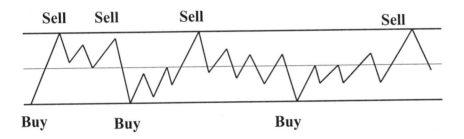

Declining Channel

We trade this pattern the same way. We short sell at the top line and we cover our short on the bottom line.

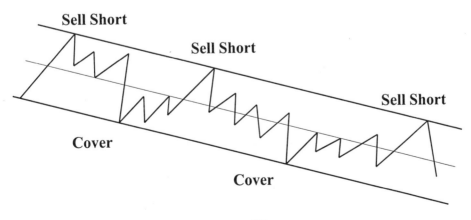

Rising Channel

We trade this pattern the same way. We buy at the bottom line and we sell at the top line.

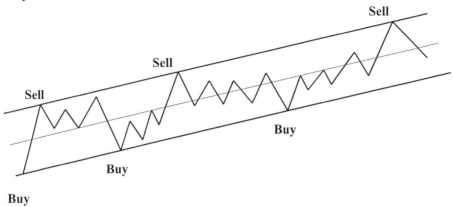

Bollinger Bands

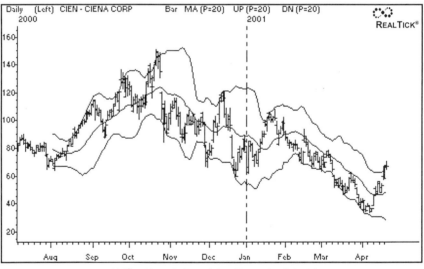

RealTick® graphics used with permission of Townsend Analytics, Ltd.

Bollinger Bands consist of three bands. The center band is the moving average for the specified period. The upper and lower bands (envelopes) are standard deviations above or below the moving average centerline. While envelopes plot fixed percentage bands around a moving average on the chart, Bollinger Bands use standard deviations to plot self-adjusting bands around a moving average. Standard deviation is a measure of volatility. This will allow the bands to increase during volatile markets and decrease during calmer periods. Bollinger Bands can be used as secondary support and resistance levels. I will show you how to set them up and how to use them later in this book.

CHAPTER 4

Where Is My Reward?

"As a trader, you must constantly evaluate the risk/reward potential of every trade and weigh it against other trading opportunities." ~ Michael P. Turner

Now that you know how I use technical analysis in my trading, I can proceed with my money management system. Let's highlight the major points of my money management system before I cover position sizing and effective stop-loss placement.

- Have a separate account for short-term trading
- Fund your account with risk capital only
- Every trade must have a plan
- The reward must be three times greater than the risk
- Diversify - Do not put all the eggs in one basket
- Never risk more than 1.5% of capital on a single trade
- Sweep the profits out of the account

These are the building blocks of a successful money management system, which is the skeleton of the *Holy Grail*. Let's learn how to utilize these building blocks in your trading system.

The following chart of XYZ might represent us with a trading opportunity. Let's see if we can write out a trading plan for a potential trade.

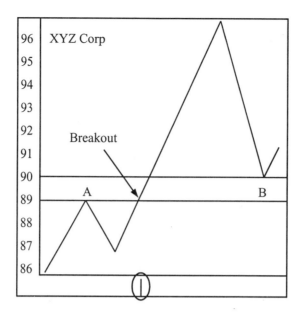

XYZ is trending upward. It made a high at 89 (A). It then pulled back to 86.75, but did not trade any lower. Investors then pushed the stock up, and it successfully penetrated the resistance level at 89 (see the volume spike) and broke out to a new high. The stock traded as high as 96.75 before selling off to 90 (B). The stock then bounced at 90 and traded up to 91.25 where it closed.

- Can I potentially find a high-probability trade for XYZ?
- If I do, what will be my entry point and price target?
- Where do I place a stop loss?
- How many shares can I buy if I have $100,000 in my account?

As you can see, XYZ is trending upward. It is making higher highs and higher lows. Next, the move up from point B might suggest that buyers have stepped back in and sellers are not as aggressive. If this is the case, then XYZ might try to test the resistance level at 96.75 again. The following are the support and resistance levels for XYZ.

Major resistance level is at 96.75 (52-week high)
Secondary resistance level is at 91.25 (the high of the last trading session)
Major support level is at 89 (the previous high the stock penetrated through)
Secondary support level is at 90 (the low of the previous trading day)

Since XYZ closed at the high of the day, I will look to buy it the next day should it trade at a higher price than the 91.25 high. This will confirm that buyers are still interested in the stock. My price target is 0.25 below resis-

30

tance, and my stop loss will be placed 0.25 below support. Let's check if my money management system will allow this trade.

Entry Price 91.40
Target Price 96.50
Stop Loss at secondary support 89.75
Stop Loss at major support 88.75

Now that I have all the numbers, I will simply plug them into my Reward/Risk formula.

Reward = 96.50 (Target Price) – 91.40 (Entry Price) = 5.10
Risk 1 = 91.40 (Entry Price) – 89.75 (Secondary Support) = 1.65
Risk 2 = 91.40 (Entry Price) – 88.75 (Major Support) = 2.65

The Tony Oz Stock Market Calculator

My dear friend, Rick LaPoint designed a special calculator to my specifications, which I use in my trading. You can download this calculator free of charge from *www.tonyoz.com*.

Since I want my reward to be three times greater than my risk, I will plug the numbers into my calculator and see if I can execute a trade based on the above numbers. If the Reward/Risk Ratio is greater than three, then it will be an acceptable trade.

TONY OZ Stock Market Calculator	Trading Plan	
Entry Price	91.40	Reward/Risk Ratio 3.09
Target Price	96.50	Potential Profit 1020.00
Stop Loss	89.75	Potential Loss 330.00
Position Size	200	

Using Risk 1 (stop loss placed at 89.75), I could execute this trade since the Reward/Risk Ratio is greater than three.

Let's see if we could use Risk 2 on this trade.

```
┌──────────────────────────────────────────────────────────────┐
│  TONY   Stock Market                                           │
│  OZ  Calculator          Trading Plan                          │
│                                                                │
│                                                                │
│     Entry Price    │91.40│                                     │
│                    └─────┘   Reward/Risk Ratio      1.92       │
│     Target Price   │96.50│                                     │
│                    └─────┘   Potential Profit    1020.00       │
│     Stop Loss      │88.75│                                     │
│                    └─────┘   Potential Loss       530.00       │
│     Position Size  │200│                                       │
│                    └───┘                                       │
│                                                                │
└──────────────────────────────────────────────────────────────┘
```

As you can see, the Reward/Risk Ratio is 1.92, which is smaller than three. Consequently, this will not be an acceptable trade.

Now that I know the maximum point loss I can take on this trade, I can figure out the size of the position I can take in XYZ stock. This is done by simply dividing the Maximum Dollar Loss (MDL) per position by the Maximum Point Loss per position. So, how many shares of XYZ can I buy at 91.40?

The maximum amount of money I am willing to lose on one position is 1.5% of my principle ($100,000), which is $1,500.

1500 (MDL) / 1.65 (Maximum Point Loss) = 909 Shares.

I can buy 909 shares at 91.40 and obey the maximum stop loss risk per position. However, if I will buy 909 shares, then I will break another rule of my money management system. The diversity rule states that I may not put more than 25% of my equity into one position, so I can only allocate a maximum of $25,000 to one position.

25,000 / 91.40 = 273 Shares.

The maximum number of shares I can buy is 273. You must remember to apply both the maximum stop loss risk per position and the diversity rule in order to figure out the maximum position size you can open.

Once the math problems are solved, I will write out a trading plan. What I refer to as a trading plan is simply the guidelines I will follow to execute a trade. These guidelines include the entry price for my trade, the price target I am looking for, the maximum I am willing to lose on this trade, the time frame I am willing to be in the trade, the size of the position I want to take, and the date in which earnings will be reported. Why do I write it all out? Because it is easier to follow a planned trade if it is written out in black and white. If the variables of the plan were not in writing, then they will just reside in my head. In which case, I could change these variables, easily. When I have it written down, I can't argue with the numbers, and I have to execute according to the plan.

In my experience, working with numerous traders over the years, I have learned that it is a lot easier to be disciplined and stick to your plan if it is written than if it is not. If you make a lot of trades on an intraday basis, make sure to write two numbers on a sheet of paper. These numbers should be your exit prices - your price target and stop loss. By writing these two numbers down, as soon as you enter a trade, you have something to follow. Writing down these numbers will help you acquire the discipline you need to be profitable in this industry.

Once you close the trade, it is important to keep a detailed record of what happened while you were in the trade. These can be analyzed later to determine which types of plays are more successful than others, and which stocks, industries or types of plays you should avoid completely. The way I like to keep records of all my trades is to include the original plan and the actual executed trade. Let's use the above trading plan in order to illustrate how I do it.

Original Plan

Stock Symbol	Current Price	Target Price	Time Frame	Entry Point	Stop Loss	Risk/ Reward
XYZ	91.25	96.50	10 Days	91.40	89.75	3.09

Actual Trade

Stock Symbol	Position Taken	Share Number	Entry Price	Exit Price	Time Held	Profit/ Loss
XYZ	LONG	273	91.37	94.63	6 DAYS	+889.98

Notes

XYZ took out the high of the previous trading day (91.25). I bought 273 shares at 91.37. I bought the stock using ARCA, and I got a reasonably fast fill. Once I was in the trade, XYZ traded down to 90.65 but never went lower. I stayed in the position for 4 days. My target price was 96.50, but the stock seemed to have peaked at 95.42 on the 4th day of the trade. I trailed my stop loss and placed it 0.75 points away from the high of 95.42 to protect profits. The stock traded lower, and my trailing stop on the ARCA ECN was triggered. My sell order was executed at 94.63.

If you read the notes carefully, you can see that I made money on the trade. However, the most important thing to me is that the rules of the original plan were never broken.

Suppose my notes were as so:

I bought 273 shares at of XYZ at 91.37. Once I was in the trade, XYZ traded down to 86.50. I stayed in the position for 4 days. My target price was 96.50, and the stock traded up to 94.75. I saw that sellers piled up on the offer on level II, so I sold the stock at 94.63. It was a perfect exit, because the stock fell like a rock from that point on. I made $889.98 on this trade.

According to the notes, I made perfect decisions on this trade. I was able to capture the maximum potential profit. Isn't that great? No, it isn't. If you read the notes carefully, you will see that I broke the rules of the original plan. I did not exit the position when my stop was triggered. I stayed in the trade and got away with it. Sooner or later, I won't get away with it, and the price I will pay will be very high.

One of the biggest mistakes is made by those who plan out their trades but lack the discipline to execute them according to their plan. This is when diverting from the trading plan will prove costly, both monetarily and psychologically. You must have the discipline to follow and execute your trading plans religiously.

Another common mistake traders make is that they fail to manage risk properly. Traders must manage risk professionally, at all times, regardless if they are starting a new position or are in a position already. Once a position is in the money, a trailing stop is another form of risk management, traders must master.

For example, let's say that XYZ stock is trading at 50. After studying the chart I have concluded that the stock is trending up, and it has a chance to go up to 56. If I were to buy the stock at 50 and am able to sell it at 56, I would have a profit of six points. After looking at the chart again, I determine that the stock has good support at 48.75, and if it fell below 48.75, I would exit my position. In which case, I would place a stop loss 25 cents below the support level. If the trade was to go against me, the most I would lose is 1.50. The risk reward ratio in this case is four to one.

The next morning, I enter the stock at 50. The stock goes up to 52.25. Can I let the stock fall all the way down to 48.50, before I exit the trade? Of course not! I have to adjust my stop loss based on risk management guidelines. These guidelines should be directly related to the reward I am seeking from the trade. The risk management rules I apply to any position are:

- Don't let a profit turn into a loss!
- Don't risk more than you can make!
- Sell at least ½ of the position at the price target!

When I say not to risk more than you can make, I mean that my trailing stop must be at a reasonable price. For instance, if my price target is 56, and the stock is trading at 55.50, then using a full point trailing-stop will be insane. I am looking to make 50 cents if I am able to sell at 56, yet I am risking a dollar in profit to try and get 50 cents. That sounds like a losing proposition to me. Once the stock gets close to the price target, the most I will risk on a trailing stop is one-to-one ratio. The reason is that I might have been conservative with my price target. In which case, I will sell half my position at the price target and give the remaining shares a chance to move higher. I will discuss this strategy and its implications later in the book.

I am sure many of you wonder about the three-to-one reward to risk ratio and want to know how I came up with that number. When I was analyzing my trading records, (trying to figure out the rewards I was getting for every dollar I risked for each one of the different trading strategies I utilize), I realized that I could expect to make about a dollar-for-dollar return on average. The formula of reward to risk ratio I featured in the chapter, *I'm sorry, but you can't take my money*, is extremely valuable to establish and modify your money management system. Once you have executed a number of trades and have enough data, you can see exactly what you could expect in returns on average, using a particular trading strategy. You can then adjust the reward/risk ratio for each one of your trading strategies.

I was doing very well in the market and felt very comfortable with my money management system. But, as I mentioned before, since my money management system had rules and guidelines, which were measured by percent, it was not flawless. In fact, when volatility increased in 1998, I had to make two major changes to my money management system.

The first change I had to make was due to lack of liquidity. When stocks are driven by momentum traders, there are either a lot of buyers or a lot of sellers.

Consequently, stocks can move up or down sharply in a less than a minute. This new market environment was brutal for stop loss order management, because you could place a stop loss order at 50, but by the time your order would get executed due to the lack of liquidity, you could lose an additional five points easily. Prior to April 1998, I was averaging an exit price that was equal to 1.73% of my equity on stop loss orders that were placed at 1.5% of equity. In April 1998, my average exit price grew to 2.68% of my equity on stop loss orders that were placed at 1.5% of equity. This was causing me a lot of grief. I had no choice but to modify the maximum percentage of equity I was willing to lose on one trade. I set that number at 1%.

After I studied the trading records in more depth, I realized that I needed to make a change to the maximum percentage of equity that can be allocated to one position. I had to also pay attention to the volatility of a stock prior to taking a position in it. This is something you will not normally find in a book that talks about position sizing. Most money management systems are just like mine was. They are simply based on percentage of equity. The problem is that if you have two stocks, XYZ and ABC, that are priced at 90, but XYZ is three times more volatile than ABC, then it will take three good trades on one to make up for one bad trade on the other. If we go back to the reward to risk formula, we can learn a very important lesson. Let's say that I can expect to make one dollar in reward for every dollar in risk on XYZ and the same on ABC, but XYZ is three times more volatile than ABC, my trading records might look like this.

Stock Symbol	Share Number	Profit/ Loss	Stock Symbol	Share Number	Profit/ Loss
ABC	300	+650	XYZ	300	+1300
ABC	300	-250	XYZ	300	-850
ABC	300	+400	XYZ	300	+1600
ABC	300	-175	XYZ	300	-875
ABC	300	+25	XYZ	300	+75
ABC	300	-325	XYZ	300	-750
Average Profit		358			991
Average Loss		250			825

As you can see in the table, although both stocks are showing me a profit overall, the average loss on XYZ stock is $825, which is 2.3 times greater than the $358 average profit I made on ABC stock. In other words, I will need to execute more than two profitable trades on ABC in order to make up for one loss on XYZ.

In order to compensate for volatility and liquidity, I made two additional adjustments to my money management system. These adjustments account for the 5-day average intraday trading range for a stock, and the 20-day average volume. I have programmed these numbers into the Tony Oz Stock Market Calculator. Let's see how you can use the calculator to determine position sizing.

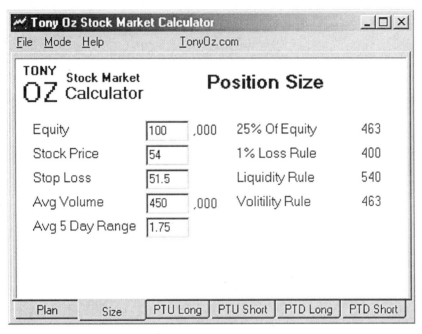

The above example shows how I use my calculator to determine the maximum position size for a potential trade. There are five fields on the left column:

- Equity (in thousands)
- Stock Price (entry price for your trade)
- Stop Loss (the exact price you would place a stop loss order)
- Avg Volume (20-day average daily volume)
- Avg 5 Day Range (5-day average trading range)

If you do not know the value of one of the last two fields, please enter "0" in that box. Once you entered all the numbers, you would use the results on the right column to determine position sizing. The **LOWEST** number on the right column (excluding zero), is the **Maximum** number of shares you may buy or sell.

If you are using RealTick®, it is quite easy to get the value of the 20-day average volume. First, you need to set up a daily chart. Next, you need to press the F9 key and select *Moving Average*. Then, click the *Parameters* button and set it up according to the following picture.

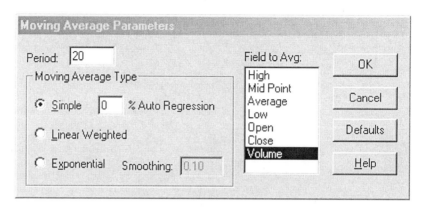

Click the *OK* button and follow by clicking the *Overlay* button. In the Panel section of the Overlay Specification window, select *Bottom* and click *OK*. The chart you have created should look like the following chart.

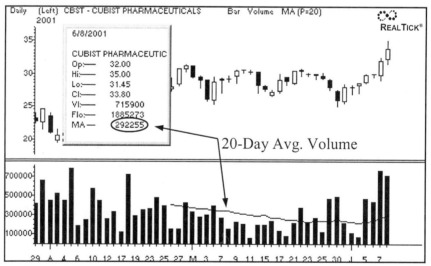

RealTick® graphics used with permission of Townsend Analytics, Ltd.

The 20-day average volume line should be present at the bottom section of the chart. If you click on any of the price bars, you should see the value of the average as seen on the above chart. This is the number you should use in the calculator.

Let's summarize the golden rules of risk management and position sizing.

- Every trade must have a plan
- Reward must be three times greater than risk
- Never risk more than 1% of capital on a single trade
- Sweep the profits out of the account

The maximum position you may take in a stock may not be bigger than:

- 25% of equity
- The number of shares under the 1% Loss Rule
- The number of shares under the Liquidity Rule
- The number of shares under the Volatility Rule

The Cost of Doing Business

Suppose I told you that I know of a trader that executes winning trades 60% of the time. This trader averages 40 cents in profit on his winning trades and 20 cents in losses on his losing trades. Could this trader possibly lose money? The answer is yes. The reason is that this trader only trades 100 shares per position. Although he makes money six times out of ten, and the amount of money he is making is twice the amount he loses on average, he is still losing money consistently. Let's do the math. Assuming that this trader executed 20 round trip trades last month, he will have 12 winning trades and eight losing trades. He would make 0.40 X 100 X 12 = $480.00 from his winning trades, and he would lose 0.20 X 100 x 8 = $160.00 on his losing trades. He will have a gross profit of $320.00. However, this trader must pay $15.00 for each trade he executed in commissions. So, for the 20 round trip trades he will have to pay $15.00 X 20 X 2 = $600.00 in commissions (2 trades make a round trip trade since we have a buy and sell order). Consequently, our dear friend actually lost $280.00 last month.

The cost of doing business is a very important element of position sizing. The following chart shows how much you would need to make on a trade of the same size in order to wipe out a loss from a previous trade. The ratio in the table tells you how much you will need to make, relatively to what you lost on your last trade, to break even. For example, if you lost 0.20 on 100 shares, you will need to make four times that loss on your next 100-share trade to break even. (I used $15.00 as commission base for this illustration).

# of Shares	Loss	Break Even	Ratio
100	0.20	0.80	4
100	0.40	1.00	2.5
100	0.60	1.20	2
100	0.80	1.40	1.5
200	0.20	0.50	2.5
200	0.40	0.70	1.75
200	0.60	0.90	1.5
200	0.80	1.10	1.37
300	0.20	0.40	2
300	0.40	0.60	1.5
300	0.60	0.80	1.33
300	0.80	1.00	1.25
500	0.20	0.32	1.6
500	0.40	0.52	1.3
500	0.60	0.72	1.2

As you can see in the table, the larger the position size is, the lower the ratio is. I use the following table to determine minimum position sizing relative to the price of a stock.

Price	Minimum Shares
Under 20	400
21-35	350
36-44	300
45-55	250
56– 74	200
75-99	150
100+	100

You must remember that all the previous rules for maximum position size apply. If by any chance, the maximum position size I can take, based on all the previous rules we covered, is lower than the minimum position size in the table on the previous page, I cannot execute a trade on that stock.

The Good

This money management system represents 15 years of experience in the stock market. It is very effective, yet simple enough, that almost anyone can incorporate it into his own trading system. It provides rules and guidelines that limit losses without hurting potential profits. When used with high-probability trading strategies, this money management system is an extremely powerful tool, and probably the most important tool for successful trading.

The Bad

This money management system is very aggressive in the sense that it allows a trader to put 25% of his equity into one stock and use margin. You must understand though that 25% of equity is the maximum I will allow for one position, but it is not the minimum position.

And The Ugly

Although maximum risk per position is set at 1%, it is possible to lose a lot more than that. A stock can trade through a triggered stop and get executed many points lower. A stock can get halted, gap open up or down 50% or more; consequently, severe losses can be taken. So, the stop loss is not the maximum risk that is taken on any trade, remember that!

CHAPTER 5

Defense Wins Championship

"We're a great football team because we play to our strengths, and we just won the Super Bowl." ~ Trent Dilfer QB Baltimore Ravens.

Super Bowl XXXV enjoyed the lowest ratings ever. In case you missed it, as the ratings would suggest you did, the Baltimore Ravens completely dominated the New York Giants. By leading its team to victory, the Baltimore Ravens' defense cemented its place in NFL history as one of the greatest units ever to play the game. A quick glance at the stat sheet shows just how dominating the Ravens' defensive performance was. They held the Giants to 49 rushing yards, allowed the Quarterback only 15 completions and forced him to throw 4 interceptions. They also made the Giants punt a Super Bowl record 11 times and did not allow them to score a single offensive point.

When it comes to stock trading, the defensive scheme of our overall game plan is our strategy to minimize loss and protect profits. Good defense is an effective management of stops. The placement of stop orders can be very tricky and extremely frustrating. However, they must be placed on every trade we manage. The question is, where?

I use the following strategies to limit my downside risk. I first take into account the risk/reward ratio presented by the setup I am going to trade. Next, I take into account the maximum allowable draw down for my position. Then, I look for the logical technical support. I use anyone of the following strategies for the placement of a stop loss:

- Below today's low

- Below yesterday's low

- Below secondary intraday support levels

- Below multi-day intraday support levels

- Below 50% retracement of last rally

- Below an index day's low or intraday support levels

Once I am in a trade in which the initial stop loss was never activated, I will use trailing stops to protect profit, which would normally be placed below logical support levels as well, unless the stock is trading at a price that is close to the target price.

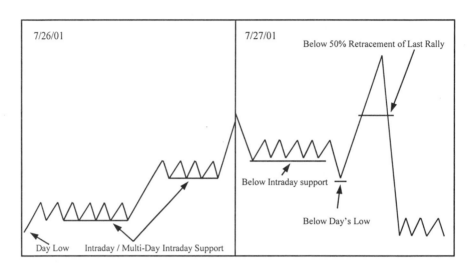

The above 2-day intraday chart shows the different strategies for the placements of stop loss and trailing stop orders that I utilize in my trading system.

In the section, *How to Find Stocks to Trade*, I feature complete trading plans for potential high-probability trades that include a variety of techniques for stop loss placement. At this point, I think it is extremely important that you become familiar with the basics of stop loss placement and understand the logic behind it.

My reward to risk formula has three variables, entry price, stop loss price, and price target. The management of any stock position I have is directly related to the value of these variables. Consequently, it is important to understand how I calculate the price target for potential trades.

Price Targets for Long Positions

Ultimately, price targets for long positions are placed just short of resistance levels. These levels can be found at previous tops or bottoms, the top of a trading channel, the upper Bollinger Band, or at one of the 20-day, 50-day, or 200-day moving averages. In addition to resistance levels, I use certain percentages of the last corrective phase as a price target. Using this method, I get three price targets, which I will illustrate in the following examples.

44

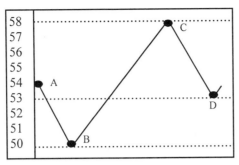

The above chart is of a stock that is trending upward. The stock made a high at 58 (C) and pulled back to 53 (D). It looks like the stock found support at 53, and it moved up to 53.75. As you should know by now, If I think the stock found a bottom at 53, and I was to buy it at 53.75, then I would have to sell the stock should it trade lower than 53.

The next thing I have to figure out is how high can the stock go from here. This answer is dependent on three different market environments, bull market, sideways market, and bear market. It is also dependent on three different approaches that I will apply to each one of the different market environments, the conservative approach, the neutral approach, and the aggressive approach. Consequently, I will have three different price targets in any of the three market environments.

Before I can proceed and forecast price targets for the different market environments, I need to figure out the value of the high and low prices of the corrective phase. Point C is the high at 58, and point D is the low at 53. Next, I will plug these numbers into my calculator.

TONY OZ Stock Market Calculator

Price Target Up Long

	High	Low	
	58	53.00	

Approach	Bull Market	Sideways Market	Bear Market
Conservative	56.00	55.50	54.75
Neutral	57.75	56.75	55.50
Aggressive	59.50	57.75	56.25

As you can see, there are three price targets for a long position in an uptrending stock for each one of the three different market environments.

Let's analyze the three different approaches for each one of the three stock market environments.

Up-Trending Stock in a Bull Market (Long Position)

The **conservative approach** is used when a stock has enjoyed a big run in a short period of time. It is also used when the market gets top-heavy.

The **neutral approach** is used when a stock is trending up at a reasonable slope. *A reasonable slope means that the trendline drawn under the low prices or over the high prices slopes within 15°-25°. You should also pay attention to the comparison between the slope of an individual stock to both the general market and to its industry.*

The **aggressive approach** is used for stocks that broke out to a 10-week high after consolidation, and the corrective phase represents a pullback from the high the stock made following its breakout move. This approach may also be used for stocks that have been in a downtrend for a while, but have now started a new uptrend. The stock must have a higher high and a higher low. (The top at point C is higher than the top in point A, and the bottom at point D is higher than the bottom in point B).

The following chart illustrated a stock that is trending upward in a bull market. Assuming the stock provides me with a high probability technical setup for a long position, which approach do you think I would use to determine the price target?

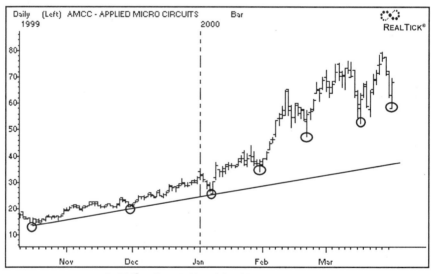

RealTick® graphics used with permission of Townsend Analytics, Ltd.

AMCC has enjoyed a gain of over 400% in six months. The stock is trading at price levels that are much higher than its trendline. The stock has been able to rally successfully and make a higher high off the last six bottoms (represented by the circles). Would the stock be able to muster a seventh consecutive successful rally? It is possible, but not very likely. Therefore, if I were to consider a long position in AMCC, I would use the conservative approach to determine a price target. Let's plug the numbers into the calculator and figure out the conservative price target for this trade. The high price is 79.44, and the low price is 57.97.

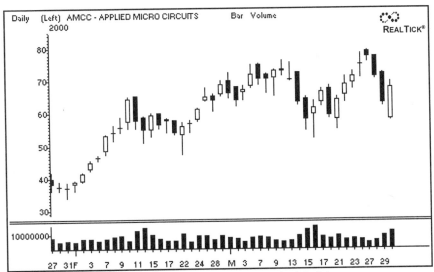

TONY OZ Stock Market Calculator

Price Target Up Long

	High	Low	
	79.44	57.97	

Approach	Bull Market	Sideways Market	Bear Market
Conservative	70.85	68.70	65.48
Neutral	78.37	74.07	68.70
Aggressive	85.88	78.37	71.93

The conservative price target would be 70.85.

Daily (Left) AMCC - APPLIED MICRO CIRCUITS   Bar Volume   REALTICK®
2000

RealTick® graphics used with permission of Townsend Analytics, Ltd.

On 3/30/00, AMCC gapped down open and raced up. Suppose we bought the stock at 61.00. We would place a stop loss at 57.72 (25 cents below the 57.97 low). Our risk is 3.28. Our price target is 70.85, so our reward is 9.85

(70.85 – 61.00). The Reward/Risk Ratio is 3.01.

After we bought AMCC at 61, it found a lot of interested buyers and traded up to 69.75. It was 1.10 away from our price target. How much lower can we let the stock go down before we would close the position? Since we used the conservative price target, we know that AMCC might go much higher than 70.85. However, one of my rules is to sell ½ my position at the price target. So, we will not risk more than 1.10 on the downside for ½ of our position. We would place the trailing stop at 68.65 for half of our position, and at 67.99 for the remaining half.

AMCC traded down to 67.28 and triggered both our stops. We are out of the trade. The stock closed at 67.97. Let's see what happened next.

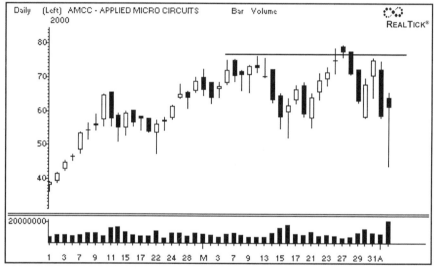

RealTick® graphics used with permission of Townsend Analytics, Ltd.

The next day, AMCC opened at 70.16 and traded down to 63.94. It then found support and managed to reverse direction. It closed at 75.03, which was more than four points higher than our price target. However, we would have been stopped out of the trade when the stock sold off in the morning. The following two days, AMCC sold off hard and hit an intraday low at 43.69. This was more than 24 points lower than where we exited the trade.

The important things to remember about this case study is both the trade setup and why we used the conservative price target approach. In hindsight, only the conservative price target would have been met, but just as importantly, had we used the other two approaches, our trailing stops would have been placed at lower prices and we would have not captured the same profits that we have captured in this case.

Up-Trending Stock in a Bear Market (Long Position)

Since we are in a bear market, the stock is moving in opposite direction to the market. This is showing strength for the stock. However, the weakness in the overall market, more often than not, will give even the strongest stock a hard time to advance in price. Consequently, the price target is lower for all three approaches. Again, I would use the same logic previously illustrated to determine which approach is the most appropriate one for a particular technical setup.

There are a few interesting things that you should be aware of. Stocks that have been laggards for a while often come to life in a bear market and advance in price. Therefore, it is not uncommon to find stocks that breakout to a 10-week high, after consolidation. It is also possible to find stocks that enjoyed a big run in a short period of time. However, expectation levels should be realistic considering the overall environment for stocks is bearish.

Sideways Market

Since there is no true direction in the marketplace, the price target is lower than it would be in a Bull Market, for all three approaches. The methodology I used to create the multiplier for sideways market is based on channel trading. When you buy a stock at the bottom of the channel, the conservative price target is normally set at the midpoint of the channel. The aggressive price target is set at the top of the channel, and the neutral price target is set at the midpoint between the conservative price target and the aggressive one. I use the same logic that I illustrated in the previous example to determine which approach is the most appropriate one for a particular technical setup.

The multiplier I use to determine the price target in sideways market is identical to all four possible trades:

- Long Position - Up-Trending Stock
- Long Position - Down-Trending stock
- Short Position - Up-Trending Stock
- Short position - Down-Trending stock

Sideways markets normally tend to move two steps forward and two steps back. Money would normally flow from one sector of the market to another fueled by rapidly changing optimism and pessimism.

Let's see how to figure out price targets for a long position in a stock, which is trending downward.

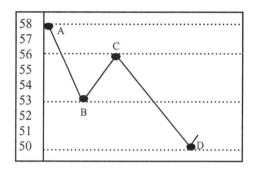

The above chart is of a stock that is trending downward. The stock made a high at 56 (C) and pulled back to 50 (D). It looks like the stock found support at 50, and it moved up to 50.75. As you should know by now, If I think the stock found a bottom at 50, and I was to buy it at 50.75, then I would have to sell the stock should it trade lower than 50. The previous low at 53 is the resistance level.

Before I can proceed and forecast price targets for the different market environments, I need to figure out the value of the high and low prices of the corrective phase. Point C is the high at 56, and point D is the low at 50. Next, I will plug these numbers into my calculator.

TONY
OZ Stock Market
Calculator **Price Target Down Long**

	High	Low	
	56	50	

Approach	Bull Market	Sideways Market	Bear Market
Conservative	53.00	53.00	52.10
Neutral	55.70	54.50	53.00
Aggressive	57.80	55.70	55.70

Down-Trending Stock in a Bull Market (Long Position)

Since we are in a bull market, the stock is moving in opposite direction to the market. This is showing weakness for the stock. However, the strength in the overall market might help the stock advance in price. Consequently, the multiplier is relatively high for all three approaches.

The conservative approach is used when a stock has just started its downtrend. The previous top made prior to point A is lower than point A, and the previous bottom prior to point B is lower than point B, as seen in the next illustration.

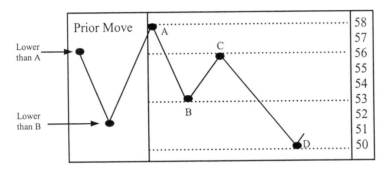

The neutral approach is used when a stock is trending downward at a reasonable slope, and has set at least three consecutive lower lows.

The aggressive approach is used for stocks that have traded down sharply in a short period of time and had at least four failed rally attempts. The support at 50 must also be a longer-term support for the stock.

Down-Trending Stock in a Bear Market (Long Position)

Since the stock is trading with the market, the multiplier for both the conservative approach and neutral approach are lower. However, the aggressive approach is actually somewhat higher. I will use the aggressive approach for stocks with long-term support at 50 that have traded down sharply in a short period of time and failed to rally at least four times. If the market also failed to rally on its last four attempts and is near long-term support levels, I might even be more aggressive. The reason is that many short sellers might get nervous and a stronger rally can emerge on a typical short squeeze. Bystanders who have been scared to participate will jump in and fall into the trap. However, it is very common to have a substantial rally after a forth leg down.

The following case study illustrates this approach.

RealTick® graphics used with permission of Townsend Analytics, Ltd.

CIEN has come down in price about 70% in 55 days. It has failed to rally four times as seen in the chart. The Nasdaq also failed to rally 4 times and was trading at price levels, which were close to 70% off its high made about 12 moths ago, and was flirting with long-term support levels.

RealTick® graphics used with permission of Townsend Analytics, Ltd.

CIEN was also close to long term support levels as seen on the above weekly chart. In this scenario, I would use the aggressive approach as my price target.

TONY

OZ Stock Market Calculator

Price Target Down Long

	High	Low	
	62.13	33.56	

Approach	Bull Market	Sideways Market	Bear Market
Conservative	47.84	47.84	43.56
Neutral	60.70	54.99	47.84
Aggressive	70.70	60.70	(70.70)

The high is 62.13 and the low is 33.56. The price target using the aggressive approach is 70.70. Let's see what happened next.

RealTick® graphics used with permission of Townsend Analytics, Ltd.

CIEN bottomed out at 33.56 and moved back up to 70.89 over the next nine trading sessions. The aggressive approach multiplier worked perfectly to forecast the price target in this case.

Price Targets for Short Positions

Ultimately, price targets for short positions are placed just short of support levels. These levels can be found at previous bottoms or tops, the bottom of a trading channel, the lower Bollinger Band, or at one of the 20-day, 50-day, or 200-day moving averages. In addition to support levels, I use certain percentages of the last corrective phase to determine price target (very similar to the previous section).

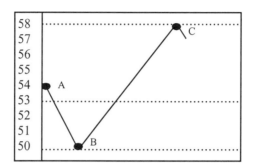

The above chart is of a stock that is trending upward. The stock made a low at 50 (B) and made a higher high at 58 (C). It looks like the stock found some resistance at 58, and it moved down to 57.25. As you should know by now, If I think the stock found resistance at 58, and I was to sell it short at 57.25, then I would have to cover my short should the stock trade higher than 58.

The next thing I have to figure out is how low can the stock go from here. This answer is dependent on the same three market environments we covered in the previous examples, bull market, sideways market, and bear market. It is also dependent on the three different approaches that I will apply to each one of the different market environments, the conservative approach, the neutral approach, and the aggressive approach.

Before I can proceed and forecast price targets for the different market environments, I need to figure out the value of the high and low prices of the corrective phase. Point C is the high at 58, and point B is the low at 50. Next, I will plug these numbers into my calculator.

Price Target Up Short

Approach	High 58		Low 50
	Bull Market	Sideways Market	Bear Market
Conservative	55.20	54.00	53.20
Neutral	54.00	52.00	50.40
Aggressive	50.40	50.40	47.60

Up-Trending Stock in a Bull Market (Short Position)

Since the stock is trading with the market, the multiplier for both the conservative approach and neutral approach are relatively low. We don't normally want to short stocks that make new highs in bull markets. However, some of these setups provide excellent opportunities if risk is managed correctly. While both the conservative and neutral approaches have a relatively low multiplier, the aggressive approach has a relatively high multiplier.

The conservative approach is used for stocks that broke out to a 10-week high after consolidation. This approach may also be used for stocks that have been in a downtrend for a while, but have now started a new uptrend. The stock must have a higher high and a higher low.

The neutral approach is used when a stock is trending up at a reasonable slope, and normally pulls back at least 50% of its last leg up.

The aggressive approach is used when a stock has enjoyed a big run in a short period of time, and it is also used when the market gets top-heavy. I would use the aggressive approach for stocks that have traded up sharply in a short period of time and made at least four higher highs. If the market made four consecutive higher highs as well, I would feel very comfortable with the aggressive approach. The reason is that investors may get nervous with the first sign of weakness and look to lock in profits.

Up-Trending Stock in a Bear Market (Short Position)

Since we are in a bear market, the stock is moving in opposite direction to the market. This is showing strength for the stock. However, the weakness in the overall market, more often than not, will give even the strongest stock a hard time. Consequently, the multiplier is higher for all three approaches.

The conservative approach is used for stocks that broke out to a 10-week high after consolidation. This approach may also be used for stocks that have been in a downtrend for a while, but have now started a new uptrend. The stock must have a higher high and a higher low.

The neutral approach is used when a stock is trending up at a reasonable slope, and has made at least three consecutive highs in a bear market.

The aggressive approach is used when a stock has enjoyed a big run in a short period of time. A bear market is never over until the strongest stocks (high fliers) get their wings clipped. I would use the aggressive approach for stocks that have traded up sharply in a short period of time and made at least four higher highs. The following case study illustrates this approach.

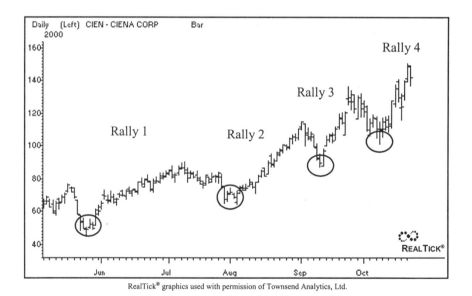

RealTick® graphics used with permission of Townsend Analytics, Ltd.

The above chart shows how CIEN made four successful rallies. While CIEN was rallying, the Nasdaq was in a bear market. If CIEN is to show the first signs of weakness, investors would most likely look to lock in profits.

56

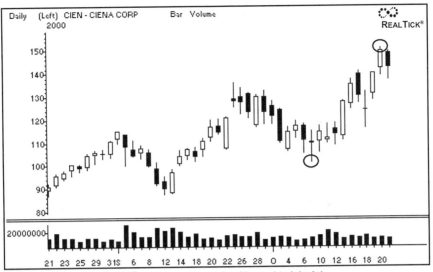

RealTick® graphics used with permission of Townsend Analytics, Ltd.

CIEN ran up from 101.25 to 151 where it topped out. The following day, the stock did not make a new high and traded lower. This was the first sign of weakness. Assuming that we were to sell CIEN short at 147, what would be the price target?

TONY OZ Stock Market Calculator	Price Target Up Short		
	High	Low	
	151	101.25	
Approach	Bull Market	Sideways Market	Bear Market
Conservative	133.59	126.13	121.15
Neutral	126.13	113.69	103.74
Aggressive	103.74	103.74	86.33

Since CIEN has ignored the market completely and has enjoyed great gains, it is very possible that the stock can sell off sharply. Consequently, I will use the aggressive approach to forecast the price target for CIEN. The high is 151, and the low is 101.25. The price target will be 86.33. Let's see what happened next.

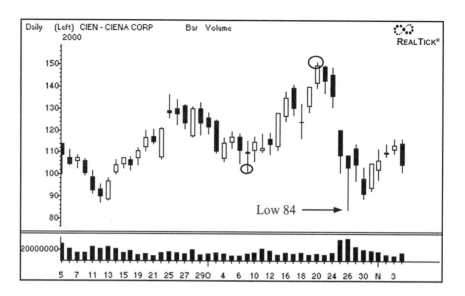

The stock went down to 84 over the next four trading days and met the 86.33 price target. Even a strong stock like CIEN will break down eventually under the weight of the market.

Now that we know how to forecast price targets for short positions in stocks that trend upward, we can proceed to learn how to forecast price targets for short positions in stocks that trend downward.

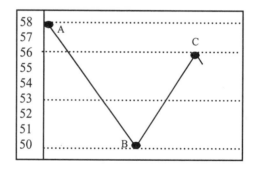

The above chart is of a stock that is trending downward. The stock made a high at 58 (A) and pulled back to 50 (B). The stock found support at 50 and traded back up. It looks like the stock found some resistance at 56, and it moved down to 55.25. As you should know by now, If I think the stock found resistance at 56, and I was to sell it short at 55.25, then I would have to cover my short should the stock trade higher than 56. The previous low at 50 is the support level.

Before I can proceed and forecast price targets for the different market environments, I need to figure out the value of the high and low prices of the corrective phase. Point C is the high at 56, and point B is the low at 50. Next, I will plug these numbers into my calculator.

```
TONY  Stock Market    Price Target Down Short
OZ    Calculator

                 High           Low
                 [56]           [50]

                 Bull        Sideways        Bear
   Approach      Market       Market        Market

   Conservative   53.90        53.00         52.40

   Neutral        53.00        51.50         50.30

   Aggressive     52.10        50.30         48.20
```

Down-Trending Stock in a Bull Market (Short Position)

Since we are in a bull market, the stock is moving in the opposite direction of the market. This is showing weakness for the stock. However, the strength in the overall market might help the stock advance in price. Consequently, the multiplier is relatively low for all three approaches.

I would use the conservative approach for stocks that have traded down sharply and are getting too "cheap" to short.

I would use the neutral approach if the stock is trading in a reasonable slope down and has rallied up to resistance levels such as the 20-day MA or Upper Bollinger Band.

I would use the aggressive approach if the stock has rallied off the lows and is hitting resistance at the 50-day MA or previous tops. I would also use the aggressive approach If I feel that the market is about to change direction and the stock has just started its downtrend.

Down-Trending Stock in a Bear Market (Short Position)

The conservative approach is used when a stock declined sharply in a short period of time. It is also used when the market gets oversold.

The neutral approach is used when a stock is trending down at a reasonable slope.

The aggressive approach is used for stocks that broke down after consolidation, and the corrective phase represents a rally from the low the stock made following its break down move. This approach may also be used for stocks that have been trending upward for a while, but have now started a new downtrend. The stock must have a lower high and a lower low.

Forecasting price targets is not an exact science. In fact, there are many variables to take into consideration prior to choosing the magic number. As I mentioned before, I feel that the ultimate approach is to use resistance levels for long positions and support levels for short positions. However, you should become familiar with the corrective phase methodology I covered as well. More importantly, you must understand the logic behind the three different approaches I have illustrated, and master the psychology behind the value of the corrective phase multiplier.

Just like everything else in my trading system, the values of the corrective phase multiplier for all the different strategies I featured in this book were fine-tuned by studying my trading records. In the future, I will keep fine-tuning these numbers as needed. Should I make any changes, I will have the newer version of the calculator available to you.

Trailing Stops

The first part of our defensive scheme is to protect the account against severe losses. We achieve this by placing initial stop loss orders, for every trade we enter, below logical support levels. The next part of our defensive skim is to protect profits. We achieve this by moving the stop loss price as the stock moves in the anticipated direction. There are a few variables that must be taken into account when we use trailing stops. The first variable is the price of the stock. The next variable is the volatility of the stock, and the last variable is the distance to the price target.

The following example illustrates a hypothetical trade:

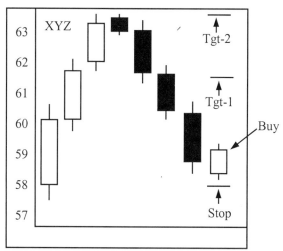

The above XYZ chart represents one of my favorite setups, which I find using my Bottom Fisher Scan. I will cover this technical setup and how to find it in greater detail later. Right now, I want to illustrate how I use stops to manage a trade.

XYZ stock made a high at 63.75 and pulled back to 58.20. The stock is up for the first time in five days and is trading at 59.10. If the stock did in fact find its bottom today, then it might be able to trade higher and meet one of my three price targets. Let's plug these numbers into the calculator to determine the price targets.

TONY OZ Stock Market Calculator	Price Target Up Long		
	High 63.75	Low 58.20	
Approach	Bull Market	Sideways Market	Bear Market
Conservative	61.53	60.98	60.14
Neutral	(63.47)	62.36	60.98
Aggressive	65.41	63.47	61.81

Assuming that XYZ is trending upward at a reasonable slope, and that we are in a bull market, I would use the neutral approach and set my price target at 63.47. Let's say that I bought 500 shares at 58.87 and set my initial stop loss at 57.95, which is 25 cents below the 58.20 low. My reward to risk ratio is 4.6 / 0.92 = 5. Let's see what happens the following day.

61

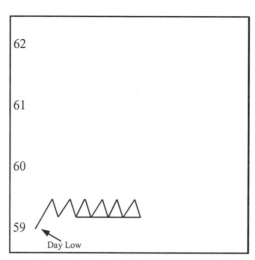

XYZ opens for trading at 59.03 and trades up to 59.44. It then establishes a trading channel between 59.25 and 59.44. Once the stock has traded for 45 minutes, I moved my stop loss to 58.78, which is 25 cents below the low of the day.

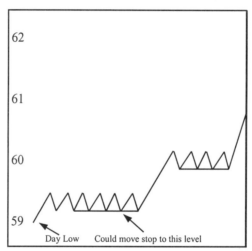

XYZ broke out of its trading channel and moved up to 60.13. At which point it started a new trading channel between 59.92 and 60.13. Once the stock broke out and moved higher, I could move my stop loss to 58.99, which is 26 cents below the bottom of the trading channel and one cent below the low of the day. An exit at this price will also assure me that I will not let a profit turn into a loss. Should I get stopped at 58.99, I would make (0.12 X 500) – 30 (commissions) = $30.00.

The stock breaks out again and closes at 60.78. This trade is showing me a paper profit of 1.91. If I am able to get my price target at 63.47, I will make an additional 2.69. However, I do not want to risk more than 1/3 of my potential rewards from this point on. Consequently, I can only allow the stock to go down 2.69/3 = 0.90. So, if the stock falls below 59.88 the next day, I will close my position. This level also happens to be below the bottom line of the channel between 59.92 and 60.13. Let's see what happens the next day.

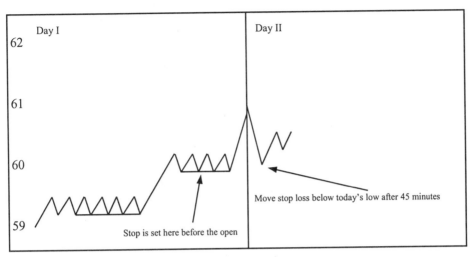

Before the start of the second trading day, I place a stop loss order for XYZ at 59.87. Once the trading day starts, I will use the low of the first 45 minutes of trading as my support level and move my stop loss there. In this case, XYZ opened for trading at 60.88 and traded down to 59.98. It then traded back up to 60.42. Since my stop loss was placed at 59.87, which is 11 cents below today's low, I did not make an adjustment to my stop loss. It was already placed at the right price.

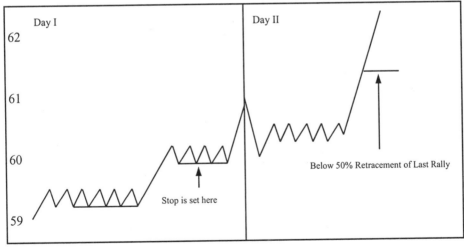

XYZ trades in a channel between 60.13 and 60.42 for about two hours. The stock then makes an explosive move up from 60.35 on high volume and hits 62.20. If the stock would be able to hit my price target, I would get an additional 1.27. If I was to only risk 1/3 of 1.27, which is 42 cents, I could easily be shaken out of my position. However, support is at a much lower level, because the stock made an explosive vertical move. In this case, I could use one of two methodologies. I could trail a stop in direct relationship to the price target I am seeking, or I could place it below 50% retracement of the last rally. If I were to use the 50% retracement of last rally, I would place my stop at 62.20 – 0.5 X (62.20 – 60.35) = 61.27, (93 cents below the high of the day). If I were to use a price target ratio stop, I would basically trail it on a one to one ratio (since the stock is over 60 and has less than 1.5 to the price target). This means that I would let the stock go down 1.27 before I exit the trade. I will make an adjustment after every 10 cents the stock trades up.

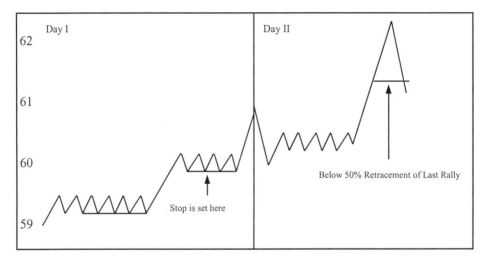

XYZ traded down and broke through the 50% retracement line. My stop was triggered and I closed the trade. I hope this example helped you understand how I use stops in my trading.

I want to take this opportunity to introduce you to the price target ratio stop loss. As I mentioned in the last illustration, the trailing stop I use is directly related to the reward I am seeking. However, it gets very tricky to use this methodology the closer a stock gets to the price target. The following table illustrates the ratios I use for stocks that are priced over 40.

% of Reward	Stop Ratio
16% - 20%	Break Even
21% - 40%	3 to 1
41% - 67%	2.5 to 1
67% - 84 %	2 to 1
85%+	1 to 1

If I was looking for a total of five points in profits, then by using the numbers in the table on the previous page, I could determine the maximum wiggle room I can give a position before exiting the trade. The following case study illustrates this methodology:

Stock Symbol	Current Price	Target Price	Time Frame	Entry Point	Stop Loss	Risk/ Reward
XYZ	50	55	6 Days	50	48.73	3.9

The next day, I bought 400 shares of XYZ at 50. My reward, if I am able to sell the stock at 55, is five points. If the stock trades in the anticipated direction, I will trail a stop loss using logical support levels. The following table represents the different prices XYZ traded at, and the price levels that represented the maximum trailing stop risk I could take, at the time, based on the price target ratio methodology.

Price	Paper Profit	% of Total Reward	Reward To Target	Maximum Stop
50.98	0.98	19%	4.02	Break Even 50.08
51.68	1.68	33%	3.32	51.68 - 1.11 50.57
52.75	2.75	55%	2.25	52.75 - 0.90 51.85
53.60	3.60	72%	1.40	53.60 - 0.70 52.90
54.35	4.35	87	0.65	54.35 - 0.65 53.70

To figure out the maximum stop, you divide the "Reward To Target" (Total Reward – Paper Profit) by the "Stop Ratio" (use the figures from the Trailing Stop Ratio Table to determine the applicable ratio).

I have to confess that I put the price target ratio stop section into the book and taken it out numerous times. The dilemma that I was faced with was caused by my fear that this methodology would not be interpreted correctly. In fact, I am afraid that readers will use the above numbers as a standard rather than a maximum. I want to make sure that you understand that these numbers represent a price level at which a stop loss must be placed, if and only if, a trailing stop below logical support levels represent greater loss. If you can find logical support levels that represent lower risk than the price target ratio stop, then you must place your trailing stop below those levels (above resistance in short positions).

The Good

The effective use of stops and price targets are essential to successful trading and longevity in this business. The elements which make the different strategies are not impossible to study and implement.

The Bad

Unfortunately, neither stop loss placement or forecasting price targets are an exact science. Consequently, you will have to deal with a lot of frustration while trying to master these strategies. However, the quality that you must have is discipline in order to execute an effective defensive scheme.

The Ugly

The following is a true story of a stock trader. "Dear Tony, since I started trading, I found myself getting stopped out a lot. I noticed that about 90% of the time the stock that I was stopped out of, went much higher. It was time to learn from my mistakes, so I said to myself that if I could find a good stock that has been crushed, I would buy it and not use a stop loss strategy. This strategy worked out great! I would watch a stock that I bought, move down pass my stop out point, then later come back up and go on to nice gains. I was happy, and said the hell with the stops, I'll never use them again. Last week, I bought what looked like a great stock that had been crushed, only to see it erode more day after day. I was down big and moved to the category of long-term investor from short-term trader. I eventually lost all my money on this stock."

CHAPTER 6

Classic Chart Patterns

There are several chart patterns such as double bottom, triple top, bear flag, head and shoulders, etc., that the professional trader can utilize in his trading system. Without exception, these patterns are based on support and resistance. However, many professionals look to trade particular patterns, so it is important to become familiar with them, learn the philosophy behind them, and understand how to profit from them.

At this point, it is important that I tell you that my methodology of trading is different than the traditional methods you might have been exposed to. **The word** *confirmation* **does not exist in my trading system!** I don't wait for patterns to confirm themselves. I act fast, and if I am wrong, I will get out of the trade immediately.

In this section, I will feature the different technical patterns. I will also show you the difference between my way of trading them and the traditional way of trading them. I will include the entry points and initial stop loss.

Double Bottom

This pattern is formed when a stock trades down to a certain price level and finds support (Point A). The stock then rallies and tops out (Point B). Next, the stock trades back down to the previous low it made, it might even trade slightly lower (Point C). That price level holds and the stock trades back up. This pattern is confirmed once the stock is able to trade at a higher price than the top of the previous rally (Point D). Another way to look at it is that a support level holds once it is tested again. A Double Bottom is also known as a "W" pattern.

Let's see how we can trade this pattern. The classic way to trade this pattern is to enter the trade once the stock trades at a higher price than Point B. A stop loss would be placed under the lows at point C. The following chart illustrates this strategy.

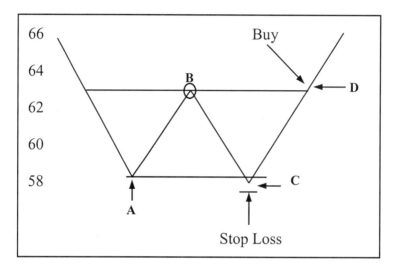

In this case, the entry price is around 64 and the stop loss is around 58. Regardless of the potential reward for this trade, the risk is six points. Although many professional traders would wait for the confirmation of this pattern and buy the stock once it trades higher than point B, I choose to buy it much earlier than that. The following chart illustrates my strategy.

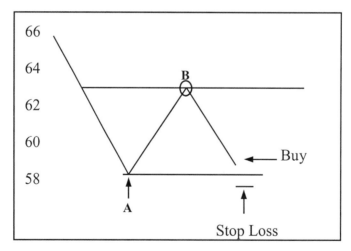

I would look to buy the stock once it is getting close to Point A. I would normally try to buy it at about 20 -70 cents (0.5%-1.00%) higher than the price at Point A. I would place a stop loss at 25 - 70 cents below Point A. My risk would range between 0.45 and 1.40 depending on the price and volatility of the stock. My initial price target would be Point B.

As you can see, there is a major difference between the way I trade this pattern to the way other professionals would. I enter the trade in anticipation of a possible double bottom formation. I am not waiting for confirmation, because the reward of entering the trade close to the previous low justifies the risk. In this case, if I used this strategy on four different occasions and my stop triggered on all trades, I would still lose less than if I utilized the other strategy and was wrong once.

Double Top

This pattern is formed when a stock trades up to a certain price level and finds resistance (Point A). The stock then pulls back and bottoms out (Point B). Next, the stock trades back up to the previous high it made, it might even trade slightly higher (Point C). That price level holds and the stock trades back down. This pattern is confirmed once the stock is able to trade at a lower price than the bottom of the previous pullback (Point D). Another way to look at it is that a resistance level holds once it is tested again.

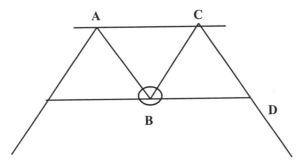

The classic way to trade this pattern is to short sell the stock once it trades at a lower price than Point B. A stop loss would be placed over the previous high at point C.

I trade this pattern exactly the same way I trade the Double Bottom pattern. I will short the stock once it rallies from point B at about 20 - 70 cents below point A, and I would place a stop 0.20 - 0.70 above point A (Point C is not known yet).

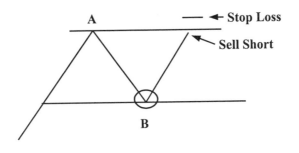

Head and Shoulders

This is a bearish pattern that is easy to spot. This pattern is considered a reversal pattern in an uptrending stock. It is a combination of three tops. The example below illustrates a typical head and shoulders pattern.

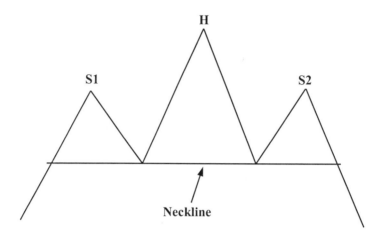

The logic behind this pattern is that investors who were buying the stock pushed it all the way up to the top of the left shoulder (S1). The stock then comes down in price to the neckline and rallies back up to a higher high (the head area). The stock then pulls back to the neckline again. Some buyers step in and push the stock price higher, this will be the top of the right shoulder (S2). However, sellers then push the stock price back down to the neckline. Once the stock price goes below the neckline a sell signal is generated.

The way I look at this pattern is that a stock made two consecutive higher highs (S1 and H). It then failed to make a higher high and topped out at S2. The stock then penetrates through support (neckline).

The classic way to trade this pattern is to short sell the stock once it trades at a lower price than the neckline. A stop loss would be placed over the high of the right shoulder (S2).

The way I like to trade this pattern is to short the rally after the breakdown. In many cases, I will use intraday support and resistance levels to determine my stops. The following example will show how I would like to enter this type of setup.

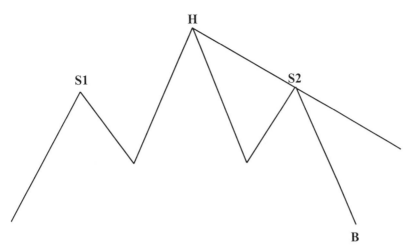

I would draw a trend line from the top of the head to the top of the right shoulder. I would look to enter a short position once the stock hits the trend line. I would place my stop loss above the high of the right shoulder. I would use the calculator to figure out a price target based on the corrective phase value from point B back to the trend line.

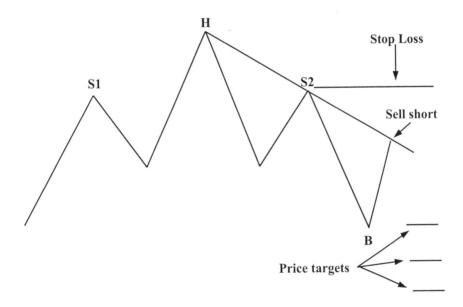

In many cases, I might use the previous day's high as a stop loss level rather than using the highs of S2. Sometime I might short a small position either at the penetration of the neckline or on the rally from point B to the neckline. I will use intraday resistance levels such as previous day's high to place my stops. As always, I look to have minimal risk and greater rewards.

The following chart illustrates a head and shoulders pattern on the Nasdaq-100 Index. The classic way of trading this pattern would have been to short the Index once it penetrated through the neckline.

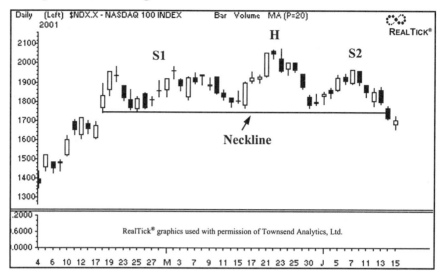

Although the penetration through the neckline is a bearish signal, you must consider the total move the Index has made from the top of S2 to the penetration of the neckline. How much lower is it going to go without a rally? That is always a hard question to answer. However, I would feel safer shorting the Index once it rallies back up to the trend line (from point H to point S2).

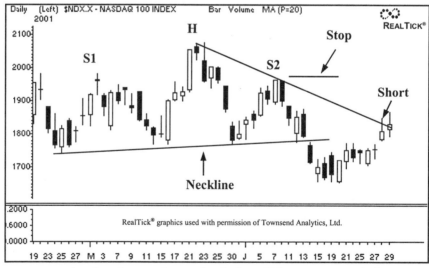

As you can see in the above chart, the Index did not go much lower once it penetrated through the neckline. Moreover, the rally following the breakdown topped the price of the neckline by more than 100 points. It would have been practically impossible to short below the neckline and not get stopped out. Let's see what happened next.

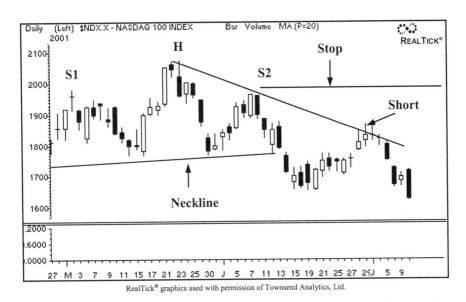

RealTick® graphics used with permission of Townsend Analytics, Ltd.

As you can see in the above chart, the index hit the trend line and traded slightly higher. If you took a short position there, your stop over the highs of S2 would have not been triggered. The Index fell down sharply in price and took out the previous lows. Now we have three consecutive lower highs and three consecutive lower lows. I don't know what happened after that, because the above chart was captured today. The last candle represents today's price action which brings me to the next example of head and shoulders patterns.

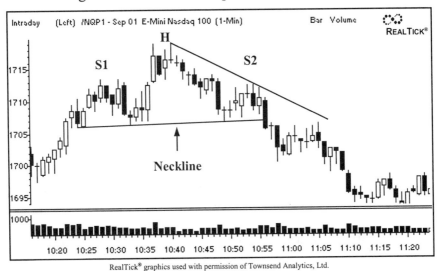

RealTick® graphics used with permission of Townsend Analytics, Ltd.

The above One-Minute chart illustrates a head and shoulders pattern on the Nasdaq E-Mini Futures Contract. As you can see, the rally attempt following the penetration of the neckline failed to reach the trend line (from H to S2). The rally did, however, reach the neckline. Consequently, if you used the trend line you would have missed the trade by one Nasdaq points. The trend line is at 1707.50 and the rally topped at 1706.50.

RealTick® graphics used with permission of Townsend Analytics, Ltd.

The above chart shows another head and shoulders pattern on the One-Minute chart of the Nasdaq E-Mini Future Contract. This time, the rally from point B failed to reach both the trend line (from H to S2) and the neckline. Consequently, sometimes you will miss a trade if you use these lines in your attempt to short the rally. This chart is of the same day as the previous chart. If you took a short position at 1706.50 or so, you would have had a potential gain of 70 Nasdaq points by the end of the day.

RealTick® graphics used with permission of Townsend Analytics, Ltd.

The above Five-Minute chart shows the price action of the Nasdaq E-Mini Future Contract for the entire day. It is important to understand that the patterns are treated the same way no matter what time frame the chart covers.

Reverse Head and Shoulders

The head and shoulders pattern can also be inverted. It can be found in down-trending stocks and it will generate a buy signal once the neckline is penetrated. This can signal the reversal of the downtrend, and a new uptrend can start.

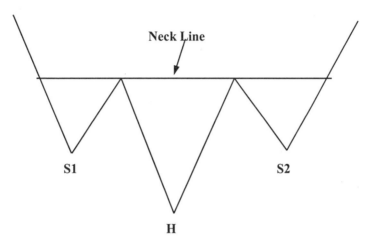

The way I look at this pattern is that a stock made two consecutive lower lows (S1 and H). It then failed to make a lower low and bottomed out at S2. The stock then penetrated through resistance (neckline).

The classic way to trade this pattern is to buy the stock once it trades at a higher price than the neckline. A stop loss would be placed below the low of the right shoulder (S2).

The way I like to trade this pattern is to buy the pullback after the penetration of the neckline. In many cases, I will use intraday support and resistance levels to determine my stops. The following example will show how I would like to enter this type of setup.

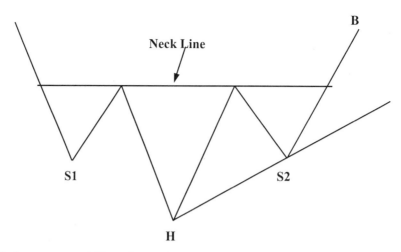

I would draw a trend line from the bottom of the head to the bottom of the right shoulder. I would look to buy the stock once it hits the tend line. I would place my stop loss below the low of the right shoulder. I would use the calculator to figure out a price target based on the corrective phase value from point B back to the trend line.

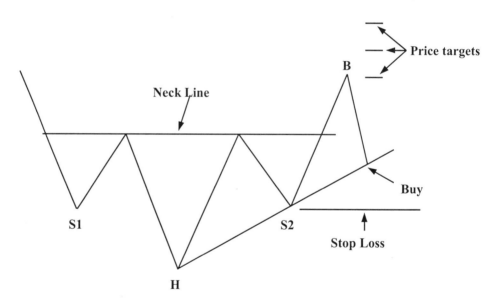

In many cases, I might use the previous day's low as a stop loss level rather than using the lows of S2. Sometimes I might buy a small position either at the penetration of the neckline or on the pullback from point B to the neckline. I will use intraday support levels such as previous day's low to place my stops. As always, I look to have minimal risk and greater rewards.

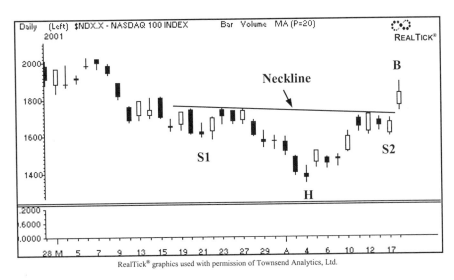

RealTick® graphics used with permission of Townsend Analytics, Ltd.

The above chart shows the reverse head and shoulders pattern the Nasdaq 100 Index formed in April 2001. The neckline was penetrated with a gap open. However, the move from Point H to Point B was very sharp and in a short period of time. Consequently, a pullback or consolidation is very likely. In this case, I will draw a trend line through Point H and point S2 and look to buy the Index should the price hit the trend line again. I will place a stop loss under the lows of Point S2.

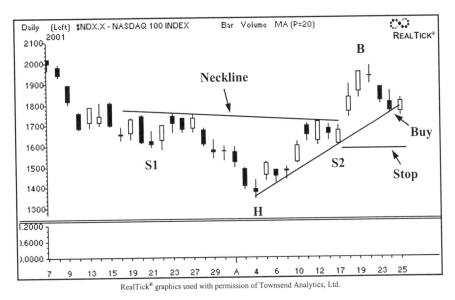

RealTick® graphics used with permission of Townsend Analytics, Ltd.

As you can see in the above chart, the Index pulled back to the trend line I drew and gave me an opportunity to buy it. Let's see what happened next.

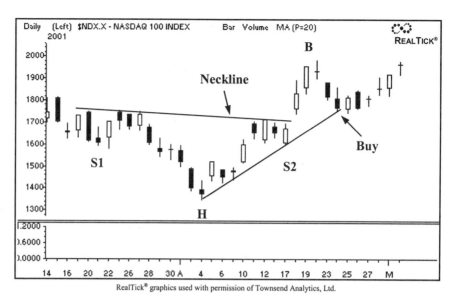

RealTick® graphics used with permission of Townsend Analytics, Ltd.

Once the Index pulled back from Point B to the trend line, it found support there. It then resumed trading up and tested the previous high. The move from the trend line back up to the highs of Point B was good for 12% over the next six trading days.

As I mentioned before, I would rather miss a trade than chase a stock and have a bad entry. I like to buy the pullbacks rather than buying the breakouts, because it gives me an incredible edge. My edge in this case is that my stop loss can be placed close enough to my entry point. This is normally impossible to do if I buy a stock when it breaks out. However, if the big picture (looking at a longer time frame) justifies an entry for a partial position at the breakout point, I might do so. I would then look to buy the pullback and complete my position. A stop loss would be placed below the lows of the pullback. I will cover these strategies in greater depth later on.

Continuation Patterns

These patterns normally represent short term consolidation or indecision between the bulls and bears before a stock resumes its movement continuing in the direction of its trend. These patterns are called triangles, flags, and pennants. These patterns can be found on bar charts that cover long period of time or very short period of time, such as a one-day, one-minute chart. These patterns are traded the same way, regardless if you analyze one-month bars on a 20-year chart, or 5-minute bars on a 5-day chart.

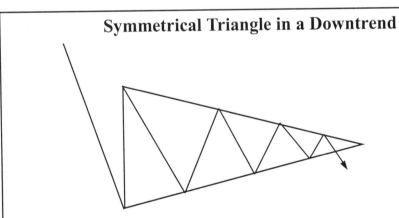

Symmetrical Triangle in an Uptrend

In an uptrending stock, if a penetration through the top resistance line of the triangle occurs then it suggests a continuation of the existing trend, hence it is a bullish (buy) signal.

Symmetrical Triangle in a Downtrend

In a downtrending stock, if a penetration through the bottom support line of the triangle occurs then it suggests a continuation of the existing trend, hence it is a bearish (sell) signal.

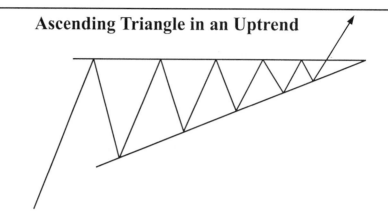

Ascending Triangle in an Uptrend

In an uptrending stock, if a penetration through the top resistance line of the Ascending Triangle occurs then it suggests a continuation of the existing trend, hence it is a bullish (buy) signal.

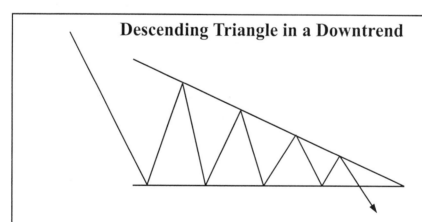

Descending Triangle in a Downtrend

In a downtrending stock, if a penetration through the bottom support line of the Descending Triangle occurs then it suggests a continuation of the existing trend, hence it is a bearish (sell) signal.

Bull Flags in an Uptrend

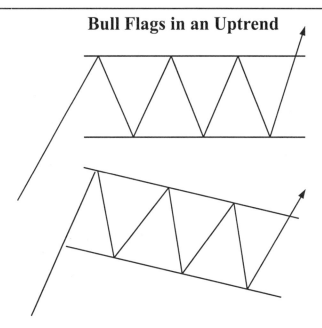

In an uptrending stock, if a penetration through the top resistance line of the Flag occurs then it suggests a continuation of the existing trend, hence it is a bullish (buy) signal.

Bear Flags in a Downtrend

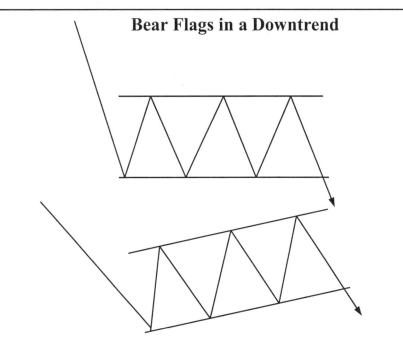

In a downtrending stock, if a penetration through the bottom support line of the Flag occurs then it suggests a continuation of the existing trend, hence it is a bearish (sell) signal.

The logic behind these patterns is that the stock is in an indecision phase. The trading price range of the stock narrows. This typically occurs on low volume. Once there is a change in the forces of supply and demand a breakout from the continuation pattern can occur. This will normally happen with an increase in volume. Once a successful breakout takes place, a continuation of the trend will resume.

This is all great, but a continuation pattern can spell "I just lost my position" to the stock trader. When you are already in a trade, long or short, the indecision areas will drive you absolutely crazy, if you follow the tape tick by tick. Remember to look at the big picture and stick to your original plan.

I find intraday continuation patterns to be of extreme value in my stop loss placement strategies. I will often use the price levels of the lows and the highs of intraday continuation patterns as legitimate levels of support and resistance, especially, if I cannot use any other price level according to my Reward/Risk formula.

I think that you should also know that I would enter a partial position many times when a stock is forming its continuation pattern rather than when it breaks out of it. I do so for many reasons. The main reason is that entering a position while the stock is in a continuation pattern gives me the opportunity to place a very tight stop loss. The reward many times is worthy of the risk. I will also do so if I think the stock would explode if it was to resolve the continuation pattern, in which case I would like to establish a partial position.

Candlestick Patterns

Candlestick charting is gaining popularity on a daily basis. Although I trade with basic support and resistance patterns, I feel that it is important to cover some of the major candlestick patterns as well. I want to concentrate on the following candlestick lines and their significance in forecasting future price movement. Since I like to keep things simple, I will only cover the patterns that I find easy to recognize and trade. All of these patterns are reversal patterns, which means that this pattern must take place in a stock that is either trending up or down, but not sideways.

Hammer

A hammer occurs when a stock opens for trading and sells off. The stock then finds support and rallies. The stock must close near the opening price. If the stock has been <u>trending down</u> for at least three consecutive days, the hammer may suggest a short-term bottom and a potential reversal of the trend. A hammer may look like this:

The tail (lower shadow) must be at least twice the length of the body for this pattern to be considered a true hammer. The way to trade this pattern is to buy the stock the next day should it trade higher than the high of the hammer. A stop loss would be placed below today's low (not the low of the hammer).

If you find a hammer in a stock that is <u>trending up</u> for at least three consecutive days, it may suggest a short-term top and a potential reversal of the trend might take place. The candles may look like any of the above candles, but the pattern is called a hanging man rather than a hammer.

The way I trade this pattern is to short a stock that is trading below yesterday's close (below the closing price of the hanging man). A stop loss would be placed above either yesterday's high (hanging man high) or today's high.

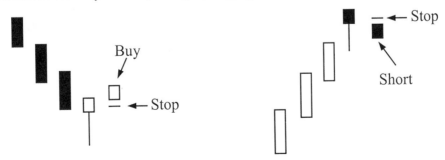

Shooting Star

A shooting star occurs when a stock opens for trading and rallies. The stock then meets resistance and sells off. The stock must close near the opening price. If the stock has been <u>trending up</u> for at least three consecutive days, the shooting star may suggest a short-term top and a potential reversal of the trend. A shooting star may look like this:

The way I trade this pattern is to short a stock that is trading below yesterday's close (below the closing price of the shooting star). A stop loss would be placed above today's high.

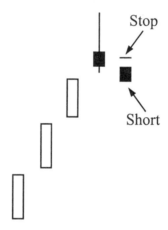

Although this pattern can signal a reversal for a stock that has been trending down for at least three consecutive days as well, I can't say that I've been as successful buying this pattern as I have been shorting it. I also found out that a shooting star does not have to take place on a gap open (as seen in the above illustration), or that the tail must be twice the size of the body. As long as there is a significant rally prior to the formation of the shooting star, the rewards can be great, as long as your entry is relatively close to the high of the day.

Indecision Reversal Patterns - Doji Lines

There can be days in which the opening price and closing price are the same. Consequently, the candlestick line will not have a body. These types of trading days are considered indecision areas and may signal potential reversals. The following examples illustrate what a Doji Line looks like.

$$\dashv \perp t \dashv \perp \top +$$

A Doji Line may look like any one of the above seven examples. What is common to all of the lines above is that the opening price and closing price for the period of time the candlestick covers are of the same value.

The way I like to trade off this pattern is to take advantage of it once it occurs after a sharp short-term rise or decline in stock prices. I trade this pattern very similar to the way I trade the hammer or shooting star patterns.

In a downtrend, the way to trade this pattern is to buy the stock the next day should it trade higher than the previous day's high (higher than the high of the Doji). A stop loss would be placed below today's low or the closing price of the Doji (not the low of the Doji).

In an uptrend, the way to trade this pattern is to short the stock the next day should it trade lower than the previous day's low (lower than the low of the Doji) A stop loss would be placed above today's high or the closing price of the Doji (not the high of the Doji).

The example on the left shows a downtrend reversal, and the example on the right shows an uptrend reversal.

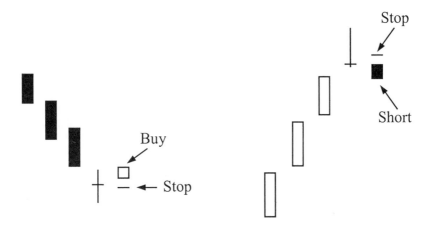

CHAPTER 7

Entry Points - Where and How

As I mentioned before, stock trading math 101 is very simple:

Good Entry = Easier Trade

Although many argue that it is **when** you sell (close) your position that counts at the end, I strongly feel that the entry is just as important. At this point, you should have a good understanding of both my overall risk management system and how I use technical analysis in my trading. You should also have a good understanding of the difference between the classic way to trade a certain technical pattern versus the way I choose to trade those patterns. In this chapter, I want to clarify where and how I enter positions.

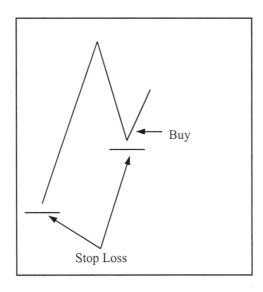

The pattern that is shown in the above **intraday** chart can be for a stock that is breaking out after consolidation (on the daily chart), or a stock that is bouncing off support levels (on the daily chart). In other words, the setup on the daily chart does not matter in this case. If I want to enter a long position, it means that I like what I see on the daily chart. I will use the intraday chart to fine tune my entry.

If I want to enter a long position, I wait for a pullback. It is important to identify the bottom of the pullback. I will enter a long position once I identified the bottom of the pullback, and I will place a stop loss below the bottom of the pullback.

If I held the stock overnight and want to add to my position, I will use the exact same strategy. I will add to my position once I identify the bottom of the pullback. The stop loss for the shares I added will be placed below the pullback's low, and the stop loss for the shares I held overnight will be placed below the low of the day.

If I held the stock overnight, and I am not interested in adding to my position, I might move my stop loss from the low of the day to the pullback's low. Of course, all the rules of trailing stop money management would still apply.

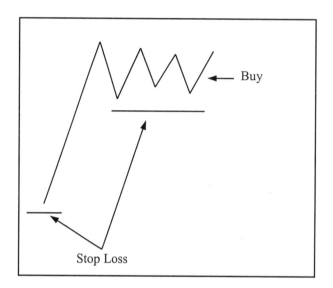

If the stock does not have a significant pullback and consolidates instead, as seen in the above chart, I will use the lows of the consolidation levels as support and place the stop loss below those lows. All the rules I used in the previous examples will apply here as well.

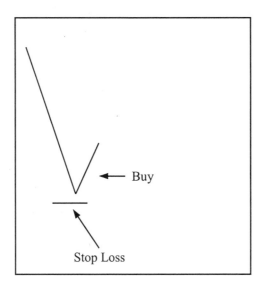

If I'm trying to catch the bottom on a stock that is trading down from the open, I will try to identify a bottom and enter the stock once it begins to rally. A stop loss would be placed below the low of the day. This would be the aggressive way to trade this setup.

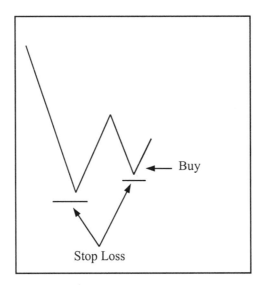

The conservative way to trade this setup will be to wait for a pullback from the rally. Once I identify the low of the pullback, and if the low of the pullback is higher than the previous low, I will buy the stock. I may place a stop loss below the low of the day or below the low of the last pullback.

If I want to short a stock, I will use the same philosophy. Let's look at the following examples.

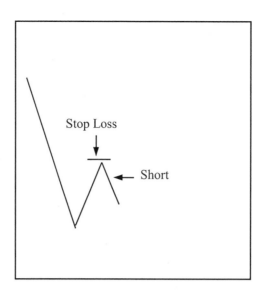

If a stock sets up for a short position on the daily chart, I will use the intraday chart to fine-tune my entry. If the stock traded down from the open, I will wait for the rally. Once I can identify a top for the rally attempt, I will short the stock. I will place a stop loss above the top of the rally.

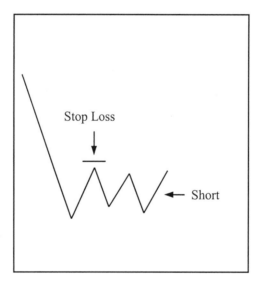

If the stock is forming a bear flag as seen in the above chart. I will short it and place a stop above the highs of the consolidation channel.

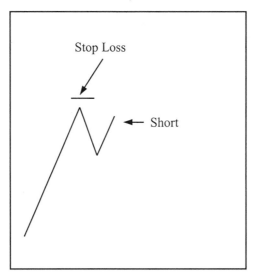

If I want to be brave and short a stock that has traded up from the open, I will wait for the first top to form and watch the pullback carefully. Once the stock rallies from its pullback, I will short it. I will try to enter as close as possible to the high of the day. I will place a stop loss over the high.

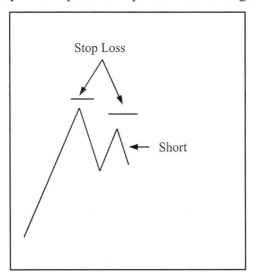

The safer way to try and short a stock that has traded up from the open is to wait and see if the rally attempt following the pullback fails to take out the previous high. If it fails to do so, then I will try to short the stock. However, since the stock is moving down, I might not get an up-tick to execute a short. Consequently, I might miss my entry. If I do miss my entry, and I still want to short the stock, I will try to short the following rally.

I recommend that you read this chapter again after you finish reading the chapters that cover real-time scans.

CHAPTER 8

The Mindset

I believe that successful trading is a product of acquired skill that combines a well-known set of proven rules and guidelines with the mindset it takes to follow and execute them. It all starts with the much-needed unconditional support from your loved ones followed by your own personal faith that you can trade stocks successfully. Then, you need to master the psychology of this business. You must have the right attitude; you must be patient; you must be confidant; you must be disciplined. You must also learn how to avoid disasters, how to keep your ego in check, how to deal with pressure, how to study and learn from your trading mistakes, how to be confidant, how to handle slumps, and what to do with profits. You should also be aware of the three devils of trading and know how to fight them, but more importantly, you must learn how to think properly in order to give yourself an edge.

Spousal, Friends and Family Support

How many people do you think would be cheerful if their better half came home from work one day and said, "Honey, I am going to make a career change, I am going to be a stock trader?" To be honest with you, I wouldn't be enthusiastic about my better half making this very same statement. However, I owe my wife a great deal of gratitude for the unconditional support she has provided me with over the years. Indeed, I truly believe that her support has contributed to a big portion of my success.

My wife knows exactly how to bring me down to earth when I am riding up so high, drunk from a successful trade I just made. But, more importantly, she knows how to say, "No big deal, you will make it back in no time," when I suffer a big loss. Her faith in me has helped me become a much better stock trader. She was supportive of me from day one, because she knew how much I loved the stock market, and she wanted me to do something that I loved.

Many of my family members and friends though, were more skeptical, not knowing exactly what I was doing day in and day out. In fact, I purposely kept them in the dark to some degree. I knew that they would be negative about what I was doing, and I wanted no negative energy around my career. I didn't think some of them could comprehend that I just lost or made more than their annual salary in one day. Don't get me wrong, I did not lie about what I was doing, I just did not share a lot of details with them. As far as they were concerned, I was an investor (venture capitalist), and I was doing computer-related work.

It is extremely important to have full support from the people you care about. If they are negative about it and tell you, "You're going to lose all your money," you probably will. To make matters worse, they will be there the day you call it quits to tell you, "Told you so, you should have listened to me!" There is nothing like having your dearest friends and family members pour salt on your wounds.

I think this issue can be resolved by the simple means of communication and education. You will have to educate the ones you care about as to the fact that stock trading is a business just like any other business, and if you are pursuing it for the right reasons, the reward will be doing something you love for a living.

I used to run into this problem repeatedly when I was interviewing potential students. They would say something like this, "I have been doing some online investing with a browser-based broker and am considering trading stocks for a living. I am interested in taking my trading to the next level by attending your seminar. However, my problem is that my spouse is not very supportive, and I feel very discouraged about it. What do you think?"

Of course, I try to explain the importance of spousal support to the potential student, but I will also try and speak to the negative spouse just to explain that stock trading is just like any other business and has the same success/failure rate. I can tell very quickly from the way the spouse reacts to hearing my voice on the other end of the phone, if the potential trader stands a chance to ever gain his spouse's approval and support. I will normally discourage a potential student from seeking a career as a stock trader if he does not get 100% support from his spouse.

Faith

You must believe that you can be successful in this business if you want to have a better chance to make it. Speculators who enter this industry without believing that they can do it successfully are making a very big mistake. I have seen these wannabe traders attend meetings of Day Traders of Orange County over the years trying to tell us all how they are considering taking on Wall Street one day, but at the same time, they don't believe anyone can actually do it successfully. They are looking for confirmation that everyone is making money and so will they, not because they have the skills, but simply because everyone else is doing well. "If they can do it, I can do it too," they tell themselves.

Please don't get me wrong, this industry is not for everyone, and by no means do I imply that everyone can do this successfully. The point I am trying to make is that if one is to enter this field, he should have faith and believe that he can do it successfully. A person who is skeptical and is looking for someone else to tell him, "you can do it," would most likely fail.

I remember an event that took place not too long ago, when someone told me straight out, "Tony, I don't believe this can be done. I want you to convince me that I can do this as well as you do." All I could do is smile and say, "Sir, as much as I want to, I can't tell you what you want to hear. It has to come from your own gut."

A seasoned trader has faith in his methodology, trading system, and all the tools he uses for his stock trading business, such as hardware, software and ISP. Faith goes hand in hand with trust. One must believe in something before he can trust it. A trader who has faith in his trading system and his ability to make calls on the market or individual stocks, will more often than not also trust himself and his system to execute the actual orders. A trader who believes in himself can trust himself to make good judgment calls on a daily basis. Good judgment calls are essential in this business.

Attitude

My grandmother Betty is an extraordinary woman, and when it comes to attitude, she is the most amazing person I have ever met. As a kid, I used to spend my summers with my grandparents. My grandmother used to work at a boarding school and was responsible for the kitchen and dining room. Everyday, over 2000 students and teachers would be fed three times. I used to tag along and go with my grandmother to work (the school had the best swimming pool and was accessible to families of the employees). I learned many valuable lessons about life from her as she dealt with work and the students who reported to kitchen duty.

If a student had a bad day, my grandmother showed him how to look at the positive side of things. If someone was furious about the duties he had to do, my grandmother would be extremely patient and in the nicest tone of voice comfort him, yet motivate him to do his duties. When her manager came rushing in screaming his lungs out at her that it would be dinner-time by the time they would be finished preparing lunch, she would smile and reply in the nicest tone of voice, "lunch will be served on time, Mr. Perez." I never saw my grandmother losing her nerves.

For years, I took my grandmother's attitude for granted. She is just the nicest person, and that's it. However, I always wondered how she did it, so I finally had the courage to ask her. To my amazement, she smiled at me and said, "I've tried to teach your mother and her siblings for years, but they took after their dad, and now you want to learn the secret, how ironic." She took a deep breath and looked straight into my eyes before she continued. "It is quite simple, Tony. Every morning when I wake up, I tell myself that I have two choices. Do you know what they are?" I didn't answer. "Well, you can choose to be in a good mood or you can choose to be in a bad mood. I choose to be in a good mood," she added. "Easier said than done," I said. "There is more," she said with that special patient tone of voice and smiled at me. "Every time a student comes to me complaining about their miseries, I can choose to accept their complaints, or I can point out the positive side. I choose to point out the positive side. Every time something awful happens, I can choose to learn from it, or I can choose to be bitter. I choose to learn from it." Although I knew my grandmother very well, I was actually shocked to hear the simple logic behind what she said, but more amazing was her strength to follow through and execute her choices while ignoring all the weaknesses we human possess. "I wish I could be disciplined enough one day to make the same choices you make," I told her. She replied, "If you remember that life is all about making choices, rather than reacting or overreacting to what it throws at you, then you will be able to choose the way you live."

I cannot say that I can control my emotions or my mood the way my grandmother does, but I can certainly say that I have improved in all aspects of the decision-making process, following my conversation with her. And when it comes to trading, I ask myself every morning the same question. Are you 100% ready to trade today? I firmly believe that the first bad trade is executed before a trader turns on his computer. A common mistake made by both beginners and seasoned traders is when they "suffer" a bad attitude phase, and they try to get even with the market. The important thing about attitude is to remember that trading is your business, and you should treat it accordingly. If you don't have the right attitude, don't trade! It doesn't matter if you are a beginner or a veteran trader. Everyday, before you start your trading program, ask yourself, do I have the right attitude today? You should know when the answer is no, and if it is no, then you should be brave enough to walk away.

Patience

Successful short-term trading consists of recognizing a high probability trade, writing out a trading plan for the trade, taking action by entering the trade, sitting patiently in the trade, and taking a profit or a loss when the trading plan tells you to. The importance of patience can be summarized as so.
Be patient and wait for a high probability set-up. Do not force trades and do

not trade for the sake of trading. Once you enter a trade, be patient and give the trade a chance to give you the reward you are looking for within the guidelines of your trading plan.

A trader must master these two aspects of patience in order to become successful and enjoy longevity in this business. If you are trigger-happy and have to execute several trades an hour, a day, or a week - sit on your hands, or tie them behind your back. There is no sense in pulling the trigger as often as some might have you believe. The professional traders I know execute fewer trades on average and are making more money, overall.

Losing is a Part of the Job

Stock traders must accept the fact that losing is a part of the job. It is unrealistic for traders to think that they can take the challenge, step up to the plate, and bat 1000. They should know that the stock market has the nastiest curve ball that will strike out the best slugger in the league. Yet, so many traders are not willing to accept that.

Stock trading is definitely a form of competition and can be compared to professional sports. Professional athletes, who are the greatest competitors, hate losing just as much as stock traders do. However, every competition has a winner and a loser, and they know that in advance. None of the players want to lose, but in order to have a decision, someone must be declared the loser at the end of the game. The main thing professional athletes are concerned with is to win as many games as possible and end up with a winning season. The professional athlete knows how to deal with a loss as long as he gives his best effort in competition.

It works exactly the same way in trading. A stock trader wants to have more winners than losers and end the season with a profit. The professional trader knows that he will lose on many trades, but as long as he enjoys a profitable season, he is doing well. Learn to deal with losses; they are a part of the job.

Trade Management

In a perfect world, a stock trader will manage all of his positions on the same merit. He will follow the guidelines and rules dictated by his trading plan and leave all the emotions out of the trade. In the real world, however, traders will often manage their current trade in an emotional way, which will be directly related to their previous trade. The emotional ties to their last trade, whether it was a winner or a loser, will dictate the action a trader will take in his current position. There is obviously a psychological effect in place, once a stock

97

trader closes a position and realizes a big profit, or a big loss. The effect is different on each and every individual trader, but the secret is to put the past trade behind you, as quickly as possible, no matter if it was a winner or a loser, and move on to the next trade with a clear mind. Successful traders often possess and utilize the skills needed to clear their mind from past trades and become 100% objective once they enter a new trade. These traders will have the discipline to stick to a well-written trading plan and follow its guidelines religiously.

Both speculators, who are just entering this field, and veteran traders, must recognize the driving force behind their decision making process. If a stock trader realizes that his decision making process, when it comes to managing an open position, is controlled by his emotions, he must make a very quick adjustment. Emotional trading is dangerous and more often than not will result in big losses. Although it is very hard to do, a trader must manage all his trades in a consistent way by following rules and guidelines that are a part of his overall trading system. Every trade should have a plan behind it. Forget about your last trade, and stick to the plan of your current trade!

Confidence

Confidence is essential to success in trading. I have worked with many students who lacked the confidence to pull the trigger. This lack of confidence was usually directly related to trust. In order to have confidence, a stock trader must trust himself to make the right judgment call. If you cannot answer *yes* to the following questions, you should not be trading stocks for a living.

- Do I trust myself to find high percentage plays?
- Do I trust myself to write out a good trading plan?
- Do I trust myself to execute my trading plan?
- Do I trust myself to enter trades?
- Do I trust myself to exit trades when I am supposed to?
- Do I trust my broker to be there if I needed help to get out of a trade?
- Do I trust that my quote feed is not lagging?
- Do I trust my entire trading set-up (computer, ISP, etc.) to perform well?
- Do I trust my trading system, its rules and guidelines?
- Can I follow my trading system and consistently make money?
- Do I understand that losing is a part of the business?
- Do I trust myself to take a loss, yet remain objective when the next high percentage trade presents itself to me?

If you can answer *yes* to all these questions, then you should not have a confidence problem. If you answered *no* to one or more of these questions, you need to work on correcting the problem, before you could exhale in this business.

Stock traders should not let losses get to them emotionally and lose their confidence as a result. Once a trader loses his confidence, he must take the steps needed to build his confidence back up before he resumes trading. A trader who loses his confidence becomes insecure. Insecure traders are more often than not very emotional and can hit a life long trading slump. Make no mistake about it, if you are lacking the confidence needed to succeed in this business, do not trade!

How to Think the Right Way

Professional stock traders know how to put themselves in a psychological advantage. A trader must know how to think the right way in order to enjoy a psychological edge. Your thought process is your best friend or your worst enemy when it comes to stock trading. Do you see the glass half full, or half empty?

It is important to learn how to think the right way in order to give yourself the advantage you need. For instance, I previously stated that a trader should sell at least half of his position at the price target he was seeking. The reason I recommend doing so is simply because the stock can go higher and a trader can capture additional gains; yet, the stock might not go any higher and by selling half the position at the price target, you would lock in profit on half the position. Let's look at this simple example and study it further.

Scenario I

I buy 600 shares of XYZ at $50. The price target is $56. The stock hits $56, and I sell 300 shares at $56. The stock goes up to $63 and falls back to $61 where the trailing stop I placed is activated, and I sell the remaining 300 shares at $61.

The right way of thinking about what took place: I sold ½ my position at my price target and captured a profit. I thought the stock looked strong, so I decided to hold ½ my position and give the stock a chance to go higher. The stock did go higher and I managed to capture five more points on half my position.

The wrong way of thinking about what took place: I sold half my position at $56, and half at $61. I was so stupid to sell at $56 because I knew the stock would go higher. I just left $1,500 on the table. Damn! I should have held the entire position and sold it all at $63. I can't believe how I left all this money on the table!

Scenario II

I buy 600 shares of XYZ at $50. The price target is $56. The stock hits $56, and I sell 300 shares at $56. The stock goes down to $54.75 where a stop loss is activated, and I sell the remaining 300 shares at $54.75.

The right way of thinking about what took place: I sold ½ my position at my price target, and captured a profit. I thought the stock looked strong, so I decided to hold ½ my position and give the stock a chance to go higher. The stock did not go higher, and I was stopped out at 54.75. In this case, I was willing to risk 1.25 points to see if I could possibly capture additional gains, but it didn't work this time. However, it was still worth the try.

The wrong way of thinking about what took place: I sold half my position at $56, and half at $54.75. I was so stupid not to sell it all at $56, because I knew the stock wouldn't go higher. I just left $450 on the table. Damn! I should have sold the entire position at $56. I can't believe how I gave away all this money!

Obviously, you can see how different the two approaches are. You will be surprised to know how many traders get so upset and see the glass half empty on a daily basis. I try to teach my students to look at things in a positive way, and not let that little devil inside of us (also known as greed) blind us from what was a good trade. This is one mistake you cannot afford to make. Learn to see the glass half full. Give yourself the psychological edge, trust me, you will need it if you plan on having a life long career in this business.

Discipline

Whenever I was talking to struggling traders at meetings of Day Traders of Orange County, I would hear a very common story. They were having a discipline-oriented problem. They did not have what it takes to pull the trigger and take profits or cut a loser when they were supposed to. I have learned something fascinating when I conducted follow-up sessions with my students. Those who were writing out trading plans were much more successful than those who did not. Those who were writing out trading plans and knew what they wanted out of a trade could exercise the discipline. Those who were not writing out trading plans and did not know what they wanted out of the trade could not exercise any discipline. Isn't that interesting?

A trading plan simply features the guidelines and rules for every trade. If a stock trader follows the guidelines of a trading plan and executes a trade according to its guidelines, then regardless if he made or lost money, he does not have a discipline problem. However, if a trader fails to follow a trading plan, then he has a discipline problem. A trader who trades without a plan, that provides him with guidelines to follow, does not have a discipline problem. How can he be disciplined if he has no guidelines to follow?

Once a stock trader has developed a trading system, which includes all the rules and guidelines such as money management, trade set-ups, etc., he must demonstrate the discipline needed to keep each and every trade within his overall trading system's guidelines. For instance, if a trader sees a stock he really likes and thinks it has a 99% chance to be a successful trade, he should not try to swing a home run and put all his eggs in one basket. He must be disciplined and follow the money management rules. Discipline applies to the entire trading system and not only to the execution of a stop loss order!

In the book, *The Stock Trader*, I featured four weeks of actual trading. I wanted to show everyone how I trade stocks for a living. At the end, I made over 55% in one month trading only the long side of stocks, and during the great crash of 2000. If readers only learn one thing from this book, it should be my strict adherence to stops. As I said in the book, "I know for a fact that my discipline in executing each and every trade according to my trading system is the secret to my success."

Taking the Blame

If you have been in the business long enough and have talked to stock traders, you must have heard horror stories of big losses a trader suffered because something that was outside of his control took place. I couldn't tell you how many times I have heard these type of stories told by numerous traders over the years. At one of the Day Traders of Orange County meetings, a trader was telling one of these stories. He told us that he took a short position in XYZ, and the next day the stock went to the moon. He wanted to cover his position, but his browser-based brokerage firm was down all day, and he could not get them on the phone; consequently, he lost his entire account. I felt really bad for this trader who caught a really bad break and lost all his money. However, a fellow trader who stood next to me, said, "I don't feel sorry for you, it is all your fault!" At first, I was surprised to hear what this guy said as it wasn't very compassionate at all, but then he said, "Tony, I am fed up with these idiots who come here and tell us how they lost all their money, and it wasn't their fault." I was listening really carefully as this guy turned to the trader who told us the story and said, "You want to know why it was your fault? Well, first you put twice the equity you had in your account into ONE stock - that is very stupid. Next, you chose to trade with a browser-based broker, obviously you did not do enough research to see what happens if your broker goes down. Finally, judging from your personality, you wouldn't have taken the loss and cut your position, because you were already down so much money in the position. You had no plan that you were trading with i.e. no price target or stop loss. Frankly, I think you were in denial the entire time and blew out your account, consequently." The trader who just got the "speech" from the guy who stood next to me, cursed at him and walked away. Then, this guy looked me in the eye and said, "I bet that I nailed it right on the head."

The moral of this story is very simple. You can't afford to make the mistake of going into denial by blaming your losses on something that was "out of your control." A professional trader takes the blame for all consequences of his trading. By taking the blame, a trader can recognize his mistakes and learn from them. If he doesn't take the blame and confess to being wrong, there is no way that he can learn the lesson.

Stock trading is a liberal profession, and it provides the trader with the freedom of choice. A trader chooses his broker, the software he trades with, his Internet service provider, the set of rules and guidelines that make his trading system, the stocks he enters, etc. Under no circumstances can a trader say, "I got into this stock because of a tip I received, and I lost because of the idiot who gave me the tip." This trader is the idiot who acted on that tip and lost on it. If you lose, it is no one else's fault but your own. When I lost a big chunk of my account on XYZ when it was halted intraday, it was all my fault. I should have known that a stock could get halted in the middle of the trading day.

Pressure

If anyone tells you that they feel no pressure when they trade stocks, check to see if they have blood flowing in their veins. Stock traders risk money on a daily basis. When someone risks money on a daily basis, he would normally be under some kind of pressure. A big mistake is made when a stock trader lets the pressure get to him and make him sick. If your stomach cannot handle this line of work, quit at once! No job is worth more than your health! I have a dear friend in Florida who used to be a floor trader. He has done well over the years, but the pressure finally got to him. He was hospitalized with bleeding ulcers and received four blood transfusions. The doctors did not think he was going to make it. However, he managed to survive and was ordered to stay away from trading for the rest of his life. It has been seven years now, and my friend is healthy. He is in the clothing wholesale business, now. He admits that he misses the action on the floor from time to time, but feels that his episode at the hospital and the survival of near-death experience has given him a second chance in life. His message to everyone who trades for a living is not to take anything into your stomach, and if you feel the pressure is getting to you, walk away, take a break and enjoy life. Stress management is key to longevity in this business. You must manage the pressure of this job in the most effective way according to your personality. Do whatever it takes and engage in as many stress relief activities as needed.

Ego

Ego plays a major role in trading stocks for a living and it represents the best and worst quality a stock trader can have. Ego is the best quality, because it takes ego to have the confidence that you can take money out of the market. You must remember that trading stocks is competitive, because we basically trade each other's money. In trading, just like in any other form of competitive sport, you need to feel, and truly believe, that you are better than your competition (even if you are not) in order to play the game. If you don't feel that way, you shouldn't even "suit-up" to play.

The flip side of it is that ego can get the best of you. When you trade stocks for a living, you have to admit you are wrong, on a daily basis. That means that when you have an open position with a loss in it, you have to close the position and realize your loss. In other words, you expected XYZ stock to do one thing, and it did another thing. You were wrong. You must lose your ego in these situations. When you are wrong, you are wrong! Close your position and move on to the next trade. Avoid the mistake of letting your ego get the best of you. Let your ego be your best friend other than your worst enemy.

Comfort Level

I remember that when I started trading, I was very uncomfortable with the idea of holding stocks overnight. In fact, whenever I held a big position, I couldn't sleep. When I finally fell asleep, I would be dreaming about my trades, and if it was a weekend, I couldn't wait for Monday to come. This definitely sounds very unhealthy, and from my work with various short-term traders over the years, I saw that I was not the only one who felt this way. However, I still held stocks overnight on a regular basis, and learned to become comfortable with that idea. I agree that some traders should not carry positions overnight, as it does not fit into their trading style, or comfort level. However, I can't stand certain training outfits that tell their students, "You should never hold positions overnight." My take on this is that a trader should definitely hold positions overnight if it fits his/her trading style and comfort level. Trading securities is about risk management, and there are scenarios where a stock has an 80%+ chance to move higher or lower the next day and closing a position just to obey the "go-to-bed-flat" rule, isn't necessarily the right thing to do. If it fits your personality and trading style, you should hold positions overnight. The rules are the same. Is the reward worth the risk? If the answer is yes, then hold your position

Winning Streaks

These are wonderful and dangerous at the same time. The positive effect is of course the fact that you are making money. The danger is that every streak comes to an end. You must exercise the same trading strategy throughout your winning streak. Do not think that you are God and can't do anything wrong. At the same time, do not get gun-shy and start trading smaller shares, because you are afraid to lose. You must keep trading the same way you have been. Do not raise your bets and do not lower them. Stay at your comfort level. The mistakes most often made by traders, who enjoy big winning streaks, is that they either get greedy or scared. They get greedy and increase their stakes exposing themselves to a big beating, which will be more devastating mentally than financially, or reduce their stakes out of fear, which will have the same effect.

For example, let's say that you have been running hot making profitable trades over a period of eight weeks. You normally trade 800 shares of stock in the price range of 44-55. You see this stock, XYZ, at $50 a share, and think it has the potential to be a winner. Let's look at a few scenarios.

A. You just cashed out of a big winning position in which you made $20,000, so you decide to buy 100 shares for fun. The stock goes down to 49, and you tell yourself, "I am only down $100, I can afford it," and you stay in. The stock goes down to 48.50, you tell yourself, "I can't be wrong on this thing," and you buy 1000 shares at that price. Stock goes down to 48, and you now say, "I know I am right on this one," and you buy another 1000 shares. To make a long story short, you are losing money and you finally can't take the pain anymore. You sell XYZ at $44. Did you have fun? Your fun trade just cost you $9,100. It is not the lost money that will hurt you. It is the psychological effects that comes with it.

B. Since you are running so hot, you decide to buy 2000 shares right from the start at 50. As you know, the stock went down to 44. It does not matter where you got out, because it will be with a loss on what is more than double your normal position. That will be psychologically devastating as well.

You can paint these two examples any color you want. The basic idea remains the same. You have changed your comfort level of trading by changing the normal number of shares you trade. You did it because you have enjoyed a winning streak. This will normally be a turning point, which could toss you straight into a brutal losing streak. This streak of losing trades will be, more often than not, a direct result of the mental damage your last trade did to you. Psychology is present in each and every trade you do. Don't forget it.

Losing Streaks

These are no fun! We all want to avoid a losing streak. Unfortunately, they do pop in every once in a while. I have explained the importance of sticking to your comfort level of trading. However, if you get off track and change the way you normally trade (successfully trade), and suffer monetary losses in the process, then you must take an immediate break to regroup! This can save you a lot of money and more importantly, aggravation.

If you lose 30% of your capital, take a break and regroup. Once you have done that, go back to trading. Do not add money back into your account. You must work with the capital you have left. Your goal is not to bring the account back to even, but to get back on track and make profitable trades. This is very important. Many losing streaks continue because of mental problems and loss of discipline. These problems arise from the simple fact that you want to make back what you have just lost. This problem is closely associated to gambling. Many traders would make the mistake of raising their bets to try and make the lost money back. This is almost always a sure way to lose a lot more. You have to remember what one unit means.

One of the hardest things to do is to adjust back to the value of what one unit means. If you make an average of $300 per trade and now you have three trades in a row in which you made $5,000 on, the next time you will have a $350 open position profit, it will not look as attractive as it did before. Why? The expectation level has changed. The same works in a losing streak. If you just lost $5,000, three times in a row, an open position profit of $400 will not look attractive either. You must never judge an open position by dollars and cents. When it is time to get out, get out! You need to make small profitable trades to build your confidence back up. Stick to your comfort level and hopefully you will get out of your losing streak quickly.

If you lose 50% of your capital, take a break again. Go over all your trading records and see why you are losing. It can be a variety of reasons, but you must be doing something wrong. It can be as simple as reading the market wrong. You must find the elements which are causing you the losses. Once you have found some answers, reevaluate your strategies. Many experts recommend paper trading again at this point. I disagree with it, because paper trading, if done successfully at this point, will not build your confidence back up. It will hurt you more in the sense that you will be upset you did not have real money in the trade. You have to trade out of a losing streak. You can't paper trade out of it. You may consider trading fewer shares at this point, but you must keep the same trading strategy you would have if you were trading a full position. If you lose 50% of your capital, you will need to make 100% on your capital to get back to the initial principle.

Regrouping After a Big Loss

Many traders make the mistake of not taking some time off after they suffer a big loss. They jump right back into trading and try to get even with the market. More often than not, they will lose more money as a result.

When I suffer a big loss or am experiencing a losing streak, I take a break and regroup. During the break I will go over my trading records and try to answer the why, what, and how questions. The thing that works best for me is to look for a trade that will take a longer time to develop. For instance, I was experiencing a losing streak in February 1999. I took my usual break and looked for a trade that could be stretched out over time. I found XYZ and from the first day I bought it to the last day I sold it, 32 days went by. I bought it in 11 different phases in the price range of 84-103 and sold it in nine different phases in the price range of 148-152. I built my position by adding to it as the stock was moving in the anticipated direction. I closed my position at my price target. This one trade made up for all the losers I had, previously. It took careful planning and execution of a well-written trading plan. The 32 days that went by helped me overcome psychological damage caused by the losing streak.

You Don't Have to Trade Everyday

Remember that you can always take a day, a week, or even a month off if the market does not look right to you. You don't have to trade just so you feel that you are working. I take many breaks when things don't look right to me. In fact, numerous times I will do all my research, get up at 4:30AM and be ready to execute my game plan, only to find out that what I was planning on doing was not doable, for whatever reason, i.e., missed an entry, big gap up or down, bad vibes, etc. When these conditions present themselves, I will call the local golf course, get an early tee time, and leave the trading desk. I do that, because I know that if I stayed around when I am in the wrong mental state of mind, I could make costly mistakes. I'd rather hit a white ball and get frustrated while scoring in triple digits than stick around when things don't feel right. The beauty of the stock market is that there are always new opportunities to make a trade. I regard this last statement as an essential element for my successful trading. It works well for me, and my wife is fine with it. This may not work for everyone, but I do believe that if you are not in the right mental state of mind, you better not trade. Remember that when things don't look right, you can just walk away. If there is something you like to do (like a hobby), you might as well enjoy that and regroup for the next trading day.

The Stock Market is not a Battlefield

One of the keys to successful trading is recognizing that the market is not a combatant. It is not a bloodstained arena, a boxing ring, a firefight, or even a physical thing. It took me years to realize that viewing the markets as a battle or a conflict or a place of adversity was not useful for my everyday psychology. Unfortunately, the pitfall of many traders is the need not just to make money, but also to be right. After spending a lot of time on this issue, I have come to the conclusion that many traders who think they are in the markets to make money are actually in it for something else.

After trading the markets for fifteen years, I have concluded that trading should be easy. The journey is hard and grueling, but once you get there, the sense of conflict and adversity should be gone. Lance Armstrong worked his fingers to the bone, but when he was leading the pack in the Tour De France I believe he was experiencing a sense of joy and focus rather than conflict or fear. Kobe Bryant or Jerry Rice would sweat and groan and knock themselves out in practice, but once it was game time, they would play in an easy flowing dreamlike state. If you want to reach that state of inner calm when trading, you must understand that trading should be fun. If you think this is a ridiculous idea, and you want to keep fighting and screaming at your monitor, you will have a hard time trying to succeed in this business.

The Devils of Stock Trading

A trader must understand that it is greed that tricks his mind into decision-making that breaks the rules. By completely understanding this, a trader ought to simply take greed and fear out of the equation. By keeping these factors out of the picture, a trader should have a mindset of playing the stock market as a game in which his only concern is to come out ahead.

I have found greed, fear, and hindsight to be the three devils of stock trading. These three devils walk together hand in hand. As soon as you are able to take greed and fear out of the picture, hindsight finds a way to bring them right back in. The problem is that it is impossible to make perfect decisions on a daily basis. A trader can never buy the absolute low and sell the absolute high. A trader can never forecast price targets to perfection. A trader can never place his stop loss at the perfect place. A trader always leaves a lot of money behind. However, hindsight finds a way to bring the would have, should have, and could have dilemmas right back into a trader's life. It is important to understand that longevity in this business is very much dependent on your ability to control these three devils. You must understand that you might not even make one single perfect decision in your entire trading career, but you could still make oodles of money. There is nothing wrong with buying high and selling higher consistently.

CHAPTER **9**

Trading Station Setup

Choosing the right tools is the first step to success as a professional trader, and it all starts with setting up your trading station. In today's marketplace, you can't expect to be a successful trader by using unreliable computers with inadequate screen space and slow Internet connection. Although personal preference plays a major role in choosing the best tools, my experience tells me that guidance is probably just as important. After all, how does one sort through all the different tools and make the best selection without any guidance? It wouldn't be easy. Consequently, I am going to share with you the mistakes I have made in the selection process and guide you to the best tools available today.

The first thing to consider is the computer that you ought to have. I highly recommend investing in the best hardware and software you can get your hands on. You should get a high-end, top-of-the-line machine, and not a low-end generic machine that can be bought from electronic chain stores or a local mom and pop computer shop. The fierce competition among computer sellers for your business has caused a sharp decline in prices. However, this sharp decline in prices comes with lower quality products, mainly low-end components such as lower cache CPUs, motherboards that limit upgrades, smaller cases that do not allow multiple video cards, etc.

Over my career, I have been guilty of buying computers from the big chain stores, local mom and pop stores, and mail-order computer builders. I am also guilty of trying to build computers on my own. I have made the mistakes, and I paid the price.

As a trader, I need a customized machine that can handle and execute tasks that are unique to trading. I need the operating system to be tweaked accordingly. I need as much screen space as possible, and I need the system to be stable. I also need customer support in case of any conflicts. It would also be great if the company that sold me the computer system were aware of any system conflicts with the latest version of my trading software.

To my delight, I found a company that specializes in building customized computers to the way I trade. The company's name is TriKinetic Technologies, *www.trikinetic.com*, and it represents a new concept in the world of computing. Each computer they build is configured for the specific trading application and support applications I run. They gather a detailed list of information about my trading platform and the Internet connection I have. Then, they use the information I give them to create the perfect trading solution for me. The guys at TriKinetic Technologies are well aware of the three major concerns I have as a trader. I want my system to be compatible, reliable, and fast! Once I receive my computer, I am entitled to unlimited free technical support, so on top of buying a computer system, I am buying peace of mind.

Next, you should definitely consider a multi-monitor setup. The desktop area is the real estate in this business, so the bigger your desktop area, the more you can see. I suggest you get the exact same monitors for ultimate results. There are two ways to setup a multi-monitor system. The first way is to install multiple video cards in a single machine, and the second way is to install a multi-monitor video card that has been designed to control more than one monitor. The biggest problem with a multi-video card setup is that there are too many variables and no standards. Consequently, conflict nightmares are the norm and not the exception. And to make matters worse, no one wants to support it. Microsoft doesn't want to support it because most of the problems are related to hardware issues. The video card manufacturers keep their distance because they don't guarantee that their cards would work with a multi-monitor setup. The box makers don't offer any support because they won't support systems that are modified from their original hardware configuration. I went through this nightmare myself. If you do not know how to set up a multi-monitor system on your own, save yourself the headaches and give TriKinetic a call. They are the specialists when it comes to multi-monitor trading station, and they will support it when other box makers won't.

When it comes to connecting to the Internet, speed is the most important thing. I don't think that a slow connection to the Internet is an option for a trader unless it is the only backup he can get to his broadband connection. I suggest DSL and cable modem as the preferred way to connect to the Internet. If you have access to both, get them both! I have had my cable modem or my DSL connection go down many times. It was well worth it to have the other as a backup. If you do not have access to either DSL or cable in your area, you must consider other options such as fractional T1 line, Satellite, moving or ISDN as the last resort. Anything less than that could potentially spell disaster.

Since I have mentioned the word backup, I should also mention the importance of power backup. Having lost power during the trading day on more than a few occasions, I learned how important it was to spend money and get a smart battery backup and high-performance surge suppression. If a power problem strikes, your computer could be rendered useless while you're managing open positions. If you are unable to restart it and get back online immedi-

110

ately, it could cost you thousands of dollars in losses. Therefore, it would be wise to buy power failure insurance.

Once you have your trading station completed, it is time to choose the best trading software that you can get. On the surface, it seems like there are plenty of choices, because there are so many products available today. However, I believe that there is only one smart choice when it comes to selecting the best trading software available today.

I think the BIGGEST mistake traders make is that they trade stocks with an online broker who does not offer Direct Access Trading to all ECNs and Market Makers. Stock traders who trade with brokers who do not offer direct access simply don't have direct access to the market! This means that they do not have direct access to the BEST possible prices to buy or sell a stock. I am amazed how many traders are out there who trade on these inferior trading platforms.

There is no way a trader should wait more than six seconds, at the most, for confirmations on executions and cancellations on NASDAQ stocks. There is also no way a trader should click the refresh button again and again to get confirmations of pending trades and cancellations. That would cost you a lot of money in the long run.

I can't tell you how many times I have seen traders try to trade stocks for a living without direct access to the market. I have seen the frustrations they face when they don't receive their confirmations in a timely manner, or when they are unable to cancel an order, or when they get a confirmation five hours after they placed the trade, and the stock went down twenty points by then. The consequences are that they lose trust in their brokers and lose their confidence at the same time. This is a mistake no one can afford to make!

If you dig into my past, you will see that I have taken this very same ride myself. I traded without direct access for a long time, and I was robbed again and again and again. I used to call my broker and get compensated for wrong doing almost on a daily basis. In one episode, I was long a stock at 10.12. The next morning, the stock opened at 15.37 and started falling down. I had a limit order to sell at 12.50 before the open. The stock traded over 12.50 for the first 78 minutes of the day. My order was marketable that entire time, but I did not get a fill. I couldn't believe it! Fifteen minutes to the close, the stock hit 10.87 and I entered a market sell order. I got a fill at 10.25. I was furious. I was not going to let this one go, and I fought it hard. The broker on the other side tried to brush me off by offering me ten free trades. I was not going to give up, and I finally reached the top guy in the firm and was compensated

$5,925. Although I was compensated for the wrong doing, I knew it was time for me to move on to direct access, because I just lost my trust in my broker. If you lose your trust in your broker, it is time to change brokers! That episode was the best thing that happened to me. It forced me to make the change, and you couldn't pay me to go back to trading without direct access.

As a trader, I need a product that offers speed, reliability, flexibility, completeness, and constant innovation. I need the product to be user friendly and be stable in extreme market conditions. This product must deliver fast reliable market data and order routing. This product must be supported by the best network infrastructure and guarantee redundancy.

Once I have completed my research and tested the different products available in the marketplace side by side, I chose RealTick®, *www.realtick.com*, as the best trading software available today. This program is put together by industry pioneer Townsend Analytics Ltd. The technology utilized in the development and implementation of RealTick® sets the industry standard for direct access trading not only for the active trader but also for institutions. Townsend Analytics Ltd. was the first to create an electronic trading platform for Windows and to offer direct access trading over the Internet. Consequently, they have had the edge right from the start, and they never lost it.

RealTick® offers direct access to all ECNs and market makers. It allows me to place stop loss orders, trailing stops and conditional orders. It allows me to use Reserve and Discretionary orders, which can be extremely valuable in many scenarios. In addition, I find the charts provided by RealTick® to be of the highest quality. They are brighter, clearer, and sharper than charts provided by other trading software. Moreover, the most important test that RealTick® passed is the reliability test. This product is by far more stable than any other trading software I tested it against. Therefore, it represents the trader with the only true solution.

If I was to compare RealTick® to other trading software, I would say that other trading platforms are like a street racecar such as Corvette, Porsche, or Ferrari. These are all great cars, and I'm sure you wouldn't mind having all three of them parked in your garage. However, if you were to race in the Indianapolis 500, do you think you'd have a chance to win the race by driving any of these three cars? Most likely you won't. Using RealTick® is like racing an Indy car in the Indianapolis 500. Using other trading software is like racing a Corvette in an Indianapolis 500 Race. If you want to give yourself a chance to win the race, then you must drive the best car for that race.

The analogy I used in the previous paragraph brings out another important point. If you never drove an Indy Car before, do you think you can just step into one and be able to race it the moment you turn on the ignition? Do you think you can go around the track at an average speed greater than 220 mph? You probably wouldn't. In fact, you would need to take some driving lessons and get familiar with the track to have any chance to succeed. Otherwise, you might kill yourself.

When it comes to using RealTick®, the most powerful trading software available today, you must take the time to get familiar with the product. You must learn how to use all the features that this product offers. This would be comparable to learning how to drive a racecar. Next, you must get familiar with all the different racetracks that you'd be racing in. This would be comparable to knowing which stock selection strategies you are going to apply to a particular market environment. In the second section of the book, I will teach you how I apply different stock selection strategies, and how I use RealTick® to execute the different strategies.

Now that we know what makes the Holy Grail of stock trading, we can answer the question that would face us as stock traders on a daily basis. How do I find stocks to trade? In the second section of the book, I will answer this question. I will provide you with numerous methods that will help you find exceptional short-term trading opportunities.

Section II

How to Find Stocks to Trade

"The average man doesn't wish to be told that it is a bull or bear market. What he desires is to be told specifically which particular stock to buy or sell. He wants to get something for nothing. He does not wish to work. He doesn't even wish to think. It is too much bother to have to count the money that he picks up from the ground" ~ Edwin Lefevre.

CHAPTER 10

News Plays

Before we learn how to find stocks to trade, it is important that we have a better understanding of the stock market. Many speculators, who enter this field, fail to understand how the market really works. They fail to understand that every transaction has at least two sides to it. They don't realize that for every dollar they make, someone has to lose more than just a dollar, (taking into account the cost of doing business: commissions, fees, subscriptions, etc.)

Another way to look at it is that we are trading each other's money. It is a competition in which there will be winners and losers. In fact, there will be more losers than winners, because of the cost of doing business. This is an industry where dog eats dog, don't you ever forget it. The trader on the other side of your transaction is trying to take your money, and of course you are trying to take his.

We are constantly searching for a set-up that will give us the upper hand. We are trying to take advantage of the changes in short-term supply and demand. That is what short-term trading is all about - Speculating on the changes in short-term supply and demand, trying to take the money from the one who misjudged it.

Every transaction has a buyer and seller. The buyer expects the price to go up and the seller expects the price to go down. This is the battle of the bulls and bears. While one buys the stock because he expects its price to go up from this point on, the one who sold him the stock did so because he does not expect the price to go up anymore; otherwise, why would he sell his stock?

Now that we know how the market really works, let's see how we can avoid disasters first.

Penny Stocks

I have not met too many stock traders who can trade penny stocks successfully. Many beginners are attracted to penny stocks, because they do not require a lot of capital. The most common mistake made by those who trade penny stocks is that they act on a hot tip or get suckered into a trade by watching unusual volume spike. In my experience, trading penny stocks does not put the odds in your favor. I will not say that no one can make money trading penny stocks, but I will say that it is very unlikely that many will. These stocks are cheap for a good reason, don't you forget that. I recommend my students to stay away from penny stocks and look for higher percentage plays. Professional stock trading is about making high percentage stock plays, and I don't feel that penny stocks provide us with good enough odds to enter them.

Initial Public Offering

Here is a call I once received from my broker. "Mr. Oz, we are the underwriters for XYZ, which is a hot stock in the Internet sector. Since you are such a valued customer of our firm, we would like to offer you the opportunity to buy shares in the company at the offering price." I was skeptical when I got this call, and I told the broker, "give me a couple of hours and I will get back to you." I started calling everyone I knew at the full service brokerage field and asked about this IPO. Amazingly, I found out that there was not a lot of demand for this "hot" new issue. I called back the broker, and I passed on his offer. The IPO was priced at $10 and opened for trading at $11.25 and immediately tanked to $8.50. I never saw it go over $10 again.

About three months later, I received another call from the same broker. He said, "Mr. Oz, we have one of the hottest IPOs ever, XYZ.com, this stock will be priced between $12-$14 a share ..." Before he could finish telling me about it, I said, "How many shares can you get me?" He answered, "How many shares do you want?" "100,000," I answered. He laughed and said, "How about 1,000?" I said, "No problem," and placed an order to buy 1,000 shares. I knew this IPO was indeed a hot one. The day XYZ was to make its debut on Wall Street, I received a phone call at 5:30 in the morning from the very same broker. "Mr. Oz, he said, we were unable to get you the 1,000 shares, however, it shouldn't be any problem, because we can place a market order to buy the shares for you, and you will be the proud owner of the stock as it opens for trading." I couldn't believe that the *snake* on the other side of the handset was trying to pull a fast one on me. I said, "What was the final offering price?" "$16," he replied. I said, "Okay, place an order to buy 5,000 shares at $16 limit." Then he said, "You know there is no guarantee we can get it at this price, if you really want this stock, you should just place a market order to buy it." At this point, I lost it. I asked to speak to his supervisor and I told her that her employee was engaging in unethical business practices by trying to convince a customer into placing a market order to buy a stock which will probably open for trading at three times its offering price. She said that he was doing nothing wrong by recommending me to place a market order if I really want to get a fill for sure. I was so disgusted that I ordered my account to be closed immediately. About six hours later, the stock opened for trading at $97 a share - a true highway robbery.

118

I knew exactly how the game the broker was trying to play with me worked. I have seen it too many times in the past. Unfortunately, there were many innocent investors who received the exact same phone call I received but did fall into the trap.

Stock traders, who place a market order to buy a hot IPO before it opens for trading, make a very big mistake. The rule is: Never place a market order to buy an IPO before it starts trading. You will not get a fill at the offering price. You will be robbed by the market makers! And if you are able to buy 1,000 shares of an IPO before it starts trading, you probably don't want them. If an IPO is really hot, you will be lucky to get your hands on 100 shares.

The next big mistake stock traders often make is trying to play the intraday swings on an IPO on its first trading day, without the proper tools. You must have the proper tools in order to play the first day on an IPO, and even with the proper tools, you are still playing with fire!

Rumor Stocks and Hot Tips

A successful stock trader makes his own play selection and knows exactly why he is in a trade. He also knows his exit points if he is right or wrong. Unfortunately, so many stock traders rely on tips and rumors to take positions in stocks. This is a huge mistake for the simple reason that the trader doesn't even know why he is in the stock, or worse yet, he doesn't know where the exit points are.

A friend of mine once bought XYZ stock, because someone told him that big news were to come out soon, and the stock would go up 50% in price. He bought the stock, and the stock started to decline in price. However, my friend could not exit the position, because he was waiting for a news release. The news never came and the stock went down 50% in price. Needless to say, he lost. I have to say that this friend of mine is a very successful trader; however, he could not have a trading plan for this trade because he was waiting for news to hit the wire. When the stock was declining, he couldn't sell his position for the simple reason that he was afraid that as soon as he would sell his position, the news he was waiting for would be released, and the stock will go up sharply. His fear of missing out on the news release cost him a fortune.

I have also made this very same mistake. Unfortunately, I made it more than once. I know exactly how it feels to be trapped in these types of positions. Notice that I used the word *trap*. These rumor or hot-tip plays are a big TRAP. You are simply stuck in a position you cannot exit. It is psychologically devastating.

119

Make your own high percentage stock selection. Plan your trades and trade your plan. Stay away from all the different types of trap plays.

News Plays

If you are a beginner and you were following my advice not to take a stock tip from anyone, then you probably would have no idea where to find stocks to trade. Consequently, you would most likely look to find stocks by reading financial newspapers and magazines or by watching financial broadcasts on TV. This should be a true agonizing experience for you as you would very likely fall in some traps called: Record earnings, missed by a penny, upgrade, downgrade, strong buy, stock picking Friday, world economy, recession, price target, Greenspan, and many more.

What I will try to do in this chapter is explain the different news related stock picking systems. I will also try to share with you some insights about the deception that professionals in this industry practice in order to take your hard earned money.

Gap Open News Plays: Dumpers and Gainers

The first method I used to find stocks earlier in my career was simply to read the news. As I mentioned before, the market initially tends to overreact to both good news and bad news. The trick was to find a situation where the good news was not so great or the bad news was not so bad, yet, the opening price of the stock reflected an overreaction. The logic behind this methodology was to buy stocks that just released bad news or short sell stocks that just released good news if there was an overreaction by the market.

This strategy requires a lot of experience and discipline. It also requires both the ability to filter through news and determine how severe or how good the news release is, and the ability to analyze the price behavior of the stock over the prior 2-4 trading weeks. Here are the rules and guidelines I follow when I use this strategy.

Long Positions

The stock, which has just reported the bad news, must be in a short-term downtrend. I want the closing price of the previous day to be at least 23% lower than the highest price the stock traded at over the last 2-4 weeks. Next, the opening price today must be at least 20% lower than the previous close. Then, I will only enter the stock if I identify buying pressure right at the open. My entry must be very close to the low of the day, and a stop would be placed right under the low of the day.

Short Position

The stock, which has just reported the good news, must be in a short-term up-trend. I want the closing price of the previous day to be at least 23% higher than the lowest price the stock traded at over the last 2-4 weeks. Next, the opening price today must be at least 20% higher than the previous close. Then, I will only enter the stock if I identify selling pressure right at the open. My entry must be very close to the high of the day and a stop would be placed right over the high of the day.

Now that you learned the first method of stock picking, I would strongly encourage you not to use it! Many of you must be wondering why I showed this stock picking system to you if I think you should not use it. The answer is that I know that sooner or later you might be exposed to this stock picking system and might want to try it. I wanted to take this opportunity to save you the heartache associated with this system.

Unfortunately, this system is very inconsistent and extremely frustrating. The entry points and exit points must be perfect. However, more often than not, it is hard to find the liquidity to get in or get out when you need to. News-driven stock plays thrive on momentum. This means that there are either a lot of sellers or a lot of buyers. As soon as the momentum shifts over, everyone tries to rush out of the door at the same time. Consequently, there isn't sufficient supply or demand to accommodate the momentum swing and give you a fill on your buy or sell order.

Another reason you should try to avoid this stock picking system is that it is strictly for intraday trading. No one wants to go to sleep at night as the proud owner of stock that just released bad news. And, no one wants to go to sleep at night short a company that just got FDA approval for a new drug. Therefore, this stock picking system is tailored to day traders only.

The main reason you should avoid this system is that it doesn't normally provide you with the greatest rewards for the time you need to spend analyzing potential candidates. Interpreting news can be very tricky, time consuming and absolutely discretionary. Therefore the margin of error is not small enough to be acceptable. Over the last three years, I probably used this stock picking method for less than 0.1% of my total trades.

Intraday News Releases

Normally, major news events are released after the close or before the open. However, there are many instances in which news can be released during the trading day. If the news is major, a stock might be halted, especially if it is a listed stock (NYSE). If the news is not major yet very important such as upgrade or downgrade, the stock would most likely remain open and trade in direct relationship to the news.

One way to find stocks to trade is to subscribe to a high-end real-time news feed and read the breaking news all day long. This stock picking system requires major skills, because you have to be able to filter through all the news that hit the wires and single out the news that you can trade on. This is extremely difficult, and I don't attempt to do it myself. However, some of the scans that I run during the day help me find stocks that have an increase in the pace of trading. More often than not, the increase in the trading pace is directly related to news. I will talk about the different scans I use later in this book.

I feel that subscribing to high-end real-time news feed and filtering through news that hit the wires all day long can be nerve-wracking for the majority of us. However, if you choose to try this stock picking method, I suggest that you paper trade it for at least six weeks before you put your money on the line. You have to keep in mind, that many times you cannot get a fill on your orders, so when you paper trade news related stock picking strategies, you must use the second best ISLD bid or offer as your entry and exit. Never use the inside market as any kind of barometer when recording paper trades.

Analyst Coverage News Plays

I will keep this short and to the point. Analysts are your worst nightmare. They are the most dishonest thieves on Wall Street. I often wonder how these guys actually sleep at night. As I said earlier in this book, I want to keep the integrity of this publication and not try to settle any scores with the firms on Wall Street. Consequently, the names are omitted from the following examples.

It is really amazing how some of the firms operate. In 1999, Firm A made millions in fees raising money for Priceline.com. Firm A's analyst, Jane Doe, recommended buying Priceline.com stock at $134 a share. When it fell to $78, she repeated her buy recommendation. And she kept recommending Priceline.com as it fell to less than $3. Not even a company's imminent collapse could force analysts to say *sell*.

On another occasion, Firm B made millions by raising most of the financing for Pets.com. Firm B's analysts, John Doe, who is paid over **seven million dollars** a year, made a buy recommendation at $16. When the stock fell to $7, John Doe said, "buy it," again. He said the exact same thing at $2 and again at $1.69. When it hit $1.43 a share, John Doe told investors to "accumulate". Pets.com was recently kicked off the stock exchange. This analyst is known in the industry as the angel of death. Every time he recommends a stock as a strong buy, he gives it the kiss of death.

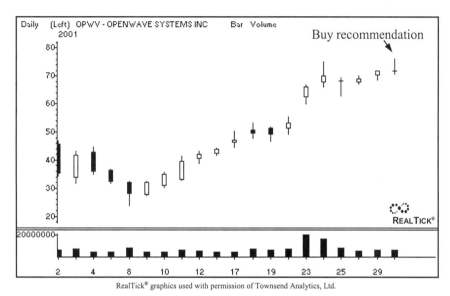

RealTick® graphics used with permission of Townsend Analytics, Ltd.

On January 30th 2001, OPWV was trading at 76. Our dear analyst, Mr. Doe, issued a strong buy recommendation and a price target of 120. I was long the stock myself and really liked it, but I knew that since Mr. Doe has just given it the kiss of death, it was time to sell it. This is what happened over the next 45 trading days:

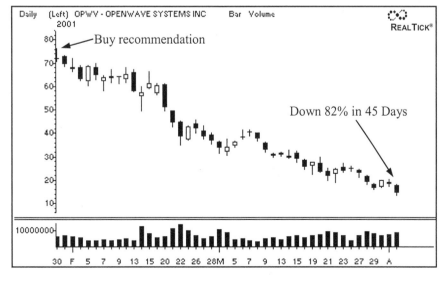

123

The stock went down to 13.51. It lost 82% in 45 trading days. In order to reach Mr. Doe' 120 price target, the stock would have to go up over 800%. Although I wasn't fooled by Mr. Doe this time and was able to make money on my position, others were not as lucky.

One of my favorite stories took place in 1998. One of the major firms on Wall Street downgraded XYZ, which traded on the NYSE. That same day, this firm was buying all the shares they could get their hands on. This was done in an obvious manner on the floor of the NYSE, and when they were asked to explain their actions, they said, "We are not doing anything wrong. This is how business is done on Wall Street on a daily basis."

The "pump and dump" way of doing business is not something that was invented by chat rooms and message boards ...

I think I could write a series of ten books on how Wall Street firms and their analysts take billions of dollars away from the individual investor. It is important to know that they only act in their best interest, and that the brokers who call clients to buy stocks from the firm's recommended list are only soldiers who carry out orders. Many of them don't even have the slightest idea of what really takes place. Since I am already criticizing them, why not tell them this: Shame on you for taking worthless companies public and initiating coverage with strong buy recommendations three weeks later, so you could take even more money from mom and pop.

TV News Plays

If you watched the TV news coverage of the 2000 U.S. Presidential Election, you should have learned an important lesson. What all TV stations have in common is that they want to be the first to air breaking news. Many times, they jump the gun.

On May 20th 1998, one of the TV stations reported that Neo Therapeutics of Irvine California had basically found the cure for Alzheimer disease. They have mentioned a story about an interview with the CEO in Italy about trials of their drug and reported that ALL 60 patients treated with the drug showed major improvements. When the market closed, the stock editor for this television stations had a special segment about this news and was practically in tears of joy reporting this story. The stock was mentioned numerous times throughout the day on this station and was the biggest percentage gainer of the trading day.

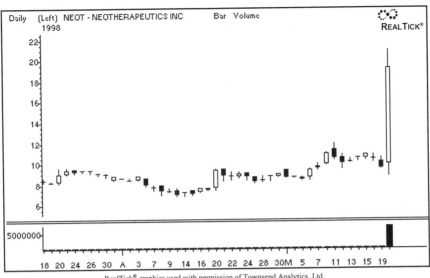

The stock went up to 21 from a closing price of 9.56 the previous day. I did the very simple math. There are over 4,000,000 people in the U.S. with Alzheimer. If they were to use one pill a day, and the pill would cost $3.00, then it would translate into 4.38 billion dollars in annual revenues. The market cap of the company was about 150 million at the time. If it were to be valued at a multiple of one times its annual revenues, the stock price would be at $584 a share. Consequently, I didn't think twice about it and bought the stock at 19.75. Although the stock was up over 100% in one day, it was trading at 97% discount to what could be a "fair" valuation. It isn't very often that you get the chance to buy 100-dollar bill for three bucks.

I couldn't sleep all night. I was so excited for the numerous Alzheimer patients across the globe who finally had hope to get over this painful disease. However, the next morning, the news wasn't so great. The CEO of NEOT had been "mysteriously" misquoted, and I ended up taking a big loss on my position. NEOT was the biggest percentage loser that day, but what was truly amazing was the fact that the television station, which pumped the stock the previous day, did not mention it even once. They did not say or explain anything that took place that day, as if NEOT did not even exist!

In the early 90's, there was a guy on this television station who had a special report. Every time he was reporting on a particular stock or sector, he was completely out of breath. I always thought that he was going to have a heart attack in the middle of his report. This guy was the king of pump and dump for his Wall Street buddies. I remember one incident when he called a $3.00 stock to go up to $12. The stock went up to $6.00 on his report, which was the highest price it ever traded at. It was a penny stock shortly after.

Once this guy "left" the television station, a new guy came along and took his place. The new guy was directly responsible for moving many stocks sharply in price in 1998-1999. He was more cautious in 2000 and 2001 probably because of all the complaints the network received. However, he still moves stocks once in a while by teasing the viewers about his upcoming report. In the meantime, the ones who know which stock he is going to talk about are buying it. Once he actually releases the report after teasing the viewer, the ones who previously bought the stock will sell it to the viewers who are watching the report and taking action. Again, the stock editor costs the unfortunate viewers money.

I recommend that you do not trade stocks that are pumped by the television networks. There are better ways to find stocks to trade, as I will show you later in this book. Remember that the guests on the different segments of the television shows are trying to push stocks that they already own.

Although it may seem on the surface that news related stock-picking systems are relatively easy and attractive, they are actually very advanced and hard to master. For instance, if a blue-chip company was to issue the following statement, "We expect the next two quarters to be tough, but we see the economy turning around in nine months or so," what do you think will happen?

- Would the stock go down?
- Would the stock go up?
- Would the market go down?
- Would the market go up?
- Would the market go up in nine months?

Unfortunately, anything can happen. If the stock and the market were "priced to perfection," then we can expect a strong sell off. If the stock and the market were "priced for disaster," then we can expect a rally. The key thing to remember is that if a company says, "we expect the economy to turn around in nine months," the stock market will go up today. Stock prices today reflect future expectations. They do not reflect the present. In other words, the market will not go down for nine months and then turn around together with the economy, if the forecast for the economy suggests a turn around in nine months.

CHAPTER **11**

Watch Lists and Sector Trading

I have three main sources for potential trades. The first one is a watch list of 30 stocks that I follow on a daily basis. This list is my Constant watch list (although I do make changes to it once in a while). The second source is sector analysis and index trading. The third source is a scan that I run during the trading day, which looks for specific criteria to be met.

When you first start out, it is really hard to know which stocks to follow. In this section I will try and guide you how to make your own Constant watch list. First, you will need to determine the criteria a stock must have in order to make it to your watch list. The most important criteria is volume. I like stocks that trade at least 1.5 Million shares. Next, I will eliminate all stocks that pay dividends in excess of 1%. Then, I will look at the volatility, which I measure by monthly, weekly, and daily trading range in points. I like stocks with large point swings. I have no prejudice against high-price stocks. I do, however, like the stocks on my Constant watch list to be over $20.00 a share. There are some exceptions though.

The best way for a beginner to start a preliminary list is by scanning for stocks that trade more than 1.5 Million shares on average. If you are a RealTick® user, you may use the following symbol chains. $ACTIVE-N and $ACTIVE-Q. These symbol chains should give you the 40 most active stocks on the NYSE and Nasdaq for the day.

Once you have created a preliminary list, your final list should be comprised of as many stocks as you could comfortably follow, on a daily basis. You should have a minimum of five stocks and a maximum of thirty on that list. When you start trading, you will make changes to the list when needed. My Constant list generates about 35% of my trades. You can find the current list of stocks that make my personal Constant watch list simply by visiting *www.TonyOz.com*.

After you have narrowed down your list, you should learn all you can about the companies that your Constant list covers. Moreover, you should know the exact price levels of support and resistance of these stocks. You should base your trading decisions for all stocks in your Constant watch list on high probability technical setups.

At the end of each month, it is important to analyze your trading performance for each stock in your constant watch list. The following example from the book, *The Stock Trader*, will illustrate how I analyze my performance.

Trading Record by Security 3/20/00-4/19/00

TICKER	P&L	TICKER	P&L
AAPL	-422..28	**MRVC**	**1,420.74**
ALTR	225.40	MSFT	99.61
AMAT	553.21	MU	597.87
AMBI	486.10	NVLS	75.00
BGEN	39.53	**ORCL**	**2,645.74**
BVSN	766.10	**PHCM**	**1,689.10**
CHKP	-50.57	**PMCS**	**1,492.10**
CIEN	**1,171.65**	**QCOM**	**-623.94**
CLRN	389.55	**QQQ**	**8,914.18**
CSCO	**1,078.73**	RMBS	-93.01
INKT	798.78	RSLC	346.01
INTC	**-754.69**	SUNW	-371.38
JDSU	-265.08	TXN	317.37
JNPR	710.82	VTSS	-581.45
KLAC	**4,625.34**	**WAVX**	**1,863.97**
LOOK	625.06	XLNX	-33.09
LSI	-170.94	XRX	561.69
MOT	-172.99	YHOO	179.47

The above table totals all my profits and losses for each stock I have traded. First, you can see that I traded 36 different stocks. Next, you can see that I turned a profit on 25 out of the 36 stocks I traded. I lost money on 11 out of the 36 stocks in the above table.

What I am interested in the most while studying this table, is which individual stocks contributed to most of my gains and which ones contributed to most of my losses. This data will help me make adjustments to my Constant watch list. There is no purpose for me to follow a stock on a daily basis if I cannot trade it well.

If you noticed, I have crossed out two stocks off the list. I use two cut-off filters to determine if I will drop a stock out of my Constant watch list. The first one is the total dollar amount which I have lost on the stock. Next, I want to see how many winning trades versus losing trades I executed for that stock.

The reason I crossed INTC out was because it represented my biggest losing stock for the month. The reason I crossed QCOM out is that I have executed three trades on the stock without a single winning trade. I lost on each and every trade I executed on QCOM. This will be the time I will say, "Good Bye."

It is really easy to keep good records if you enter all your trades into a program such as Quicken. My broker has made my life much easier, because they create a Quicken file for their customers, on a daily basis. I can download and import this file into my program at my convenience. Once I have all the data imported to Quicken, I can generate reports and graphs that give me a clear picture of my trading performance.

Exchange Traded Funds

The second source I have for potential trades is index and sector trading. This method of trading can be done by creating and trading a basket of stocks, or by trading an ETF.

Listed on different exchanges and traded in the open Market is an entire family of Exchange Traded Funds (ETF). These index-based investment products let you buy or sell shares of entire portfolios of stock in a single security. Pioneered by the Amex, these unique financial products combine the opportunities of indexing with the advantages of stock trading. There are three ETFs that can easily be traded:

DIA: The DIAMONDS Trust Series is a pooled investment designed to provide investment results that generally correspond to the price and yield performance of the Dow Jones Industrial Average.

SPY: The SPDR Trust Series is a pooled investment designed to provide investment results that generally correspond to the price and yield performance

129

of the S&P 500 index.

QQQ: The Nasdaq-100 Trust Series is a pooled investment designed to provide investment results that generally correspond to the price and yield performance of the Nasdaq-100 index.

I swing trade any of the above three ETFs frequently. I use the same support and resistance concepts and look for defined trading channels before I enter positions. The time frame for the swing trades is somewhat longer in trending markets than it would be for an individual company stock.

Sector Trading

Due to the constant shift of institutional money from one sector to another, a trader must know which sector is getting hot and which sector is getting cold. If money is rotated out of the tech and Internet stocks, it needs to go somewhere else; consequently, another sector of the market will get new interest. Some days there may be strength in the oil stocks, and in other days, the pharmaceutical stocks might be strong. The point is that there is always going to be one or two sectors that are better to trade than others.

There are two ways to trade a sector of the market. The first is by trading HOLDRS, which are trust–issued receipts that represent ownership of a specified group of stocks or by creating and trading baskets. HOLDRS automatically provide the investor with diversified exposure to an industry, sector, or group of stocks in a single investment. These can be traded in a similar fashion to ETF. However, many HOLDRS are thinly traded, so you must be careful. The following table shows the available HOLDRS as of 5/31/01.

Ticker	Name
BBH	Biotech HOLDRS
BDH	Broadband HOLDRS
BHH	B2B Internet HOLDRS
EKH	Europe 2001 Holdrs
HHH	Internet HOLDRS
IAH	Internet Architecture ...
IIH	Internet Infrastructure
MKH	Market 2000+ Holdrs
OIH	Oil Svc Holdrs
PPH	Pharmaceutical HOLDRS
RKH	Regional Bank HOLDRS
RTH	Retail Holdrs Tr
SMH	Semiconductor HOLDRS
SWH	Software Holdrs
TBH	Telecomunicacoes Brasil
TTH	Telecom HOLDRS
UTH	Utilities HOLDRS
WMH	Wireless Holdrs

Basket Trading

The second way to trade a sector of the market is by creating baskets of stocks that belong to a particular sector or industry on your own. What I try to do is to find the strongest sector and buy the strongest stocks in that sector. I try to create a "basket" of stocks that will outperform both the market and the sector they belong to. For my stock selection criteria, I simply look for the most known liquid names. Here is how I manage a basket position. As the index goes up, I sell the stocks in the basket that are going down or are flat. This permits me to stay in only the stocks that are going up. When the index turns down and violates support levels, I will liquidate the entire basket. Since I hold a group of stocks in the same sector, my position window, which updates dynamically with every tick, gives me a "real-time" view of what is taking place. My open P&L tracks the changes in bid prices for the entire basket. I have featured the advantages and disadvantages of trading baskets of stocks that track certain sectors. The following are baskets of stocks which I have created for the purpose of trading a hot sector. You may want to visit *www.TonyOz.com* for the latest and most current list.

BIOTECH
IMNX, AMGN, BGEN, MEDI, PDLI

COMPUTER MAKERS
DELL, CPQ, SUNW, IBM, HWP, AAPL, GTW, MU

INTERNET
AOL, YHOO, CMGI, DCLK, VRSN, AMZN, RNWK, EBAY, CHKP, INKT, BVSN

CYCLICAL STOCKS
C, DE, F, IP, CHA, AA, UK, UTX, HON, CAT, GT, DOW

TELECOM
T, WCOM, NT, LU, BEL, NXTL, SBC, PCS, GTE, USW, FON

NETWORK
CSCO, NT, LU, COMS, TLAB, CIEN, ADCT, ADPT, CS, ALA, NN

OIL SERVICES
HAL, SLB, BHI, RIG, GLM, FLC, TDW, NE, MAVK, CHV, RD

PHARMACUITICLES
PFE, AMGN, SGP, LLY, MRK, BMY, ABT, WLA, AHP, JNJ

BROKERS
SCH, MER, LEH, GS, PWJ, MWD

AIRLINES
AMR, DAL, NWAC, ALK, UAL

SEMICONDUCTORS
INTC, AMAT, MOT, MU, KLAC, PMCS, LSI, TXN, ALTR, NVLS, AMD

CHAPTER 12

Real-Time Scans

So far, we have learned two effective stock picking methods. The first is creating a Constant watch list and trading stocks from that list, and the second is index and sector trading. Both of these methods can be extremely profitable. However, the greatest profits and the greatest reward to risk setups are often found by using my third method of stock picking. The following chapters will cover this method in great detail. If you master these chapters, you most likely won't have to ask the question, how do I find stocks to trade?

The Oz Scanner

With over 12,000 stocks to look at every day, I use a state-of-the-art technical scanning tool to quickly and effectively find stocks to trade. The scanner applies technical screening formulas to a large population of stocks. It then returns a list of stocks that meet pre-determined filter criteria associated with those formulas, culled throughout the trading day. Once I receive the list of stocks generated by the scanner, I then proceed to evaluate potential risk and potential reward prior to establishing a position in the stock.

I developed these scans because I was constantly trying to find better-than-average stock trading opportunities, and sought an automated means to this end. The decision of which stock to trade next was the dilemma I faced every time I closed a trade. If I wanted to quickly find the next fast-moving or slow-moving stocks with better-than-average upside or downside potential, I was simply out of luck. Consequently, I developed a product that would put these stocks in front of my eyes.

All of my scans are designed with a particular trading philosophy in mind. For instance, my Bottom Fisher scan tries to find weak stocks that are showing signs of an intraday turnaround, or strong stocks that have been correcting and are now ready to resume their longer-term trends. Another example is my New Kid on the Block Scan, which tries to find up-and-coming stocks that are moving higher on increasing trading volume.

Before I get into the specifics of each pre-defined scan, and how to use them, I must make sure that you are clear on the following issues. First, if you decide to use these strategies and incorporate them into your trading system, you must understand that my scans are alerting you to stocks which meet certain criteria and may **potentially** present a trading opportunity. However, not every result on the list represents a high-probability trade. In fact, the alerts should not be traded blindly. Understand the dynamics of the move you seek, in order to determine which of the scanned stocks best meets your personal trading needs. Next, you must understand that although my scans are well designed to filter out many stocks that are not in a very "promising" position, it doesn't necessarily mean that all stocks returned by the scans will be useful to the user. In order to get the most out of this stock picking method, I recommend that you consider the following guidelines.

- Determine your trading style: Which technical setups are you most comfortable with? What is your risk management system? Which scans are tailored to your overall trading system and personality?

- Determine your time frame: Are you looking for short-term or long-term opportunities? Are you looking for intraday trades, exclusively?

- Understand the philosophy behind the scans: Do you understand what each scan is searching for? Do you understand what the scanner is filtering out? Do you understand the strategies and risk management to be applied to each individual scan. Can you filter through the results and select the most promising ones?

- Review the charts of all the stocks selected by the scan prior to taking a position: Does the stock selected by the scan have a chart that looks promising to you? How many charts look promising? How many stocks can you track at the same time?

- Paper-trade the strategies first: Are you profitable trading these strategies on paper? Do you feel confidant that you can have positive results if you have real money on the line? After tracking the results for several trading periods, how many of the "promising" stocks actually moved in profitable ways? Would any of the unprofitable stocks have caused you to lose more than you are willing to risk in the market?

After a while, you should begin to recognize repeated patterns in the behavior of stocks that a particular scan selects. It is very important to develop a sense for finding the stocks that may repeat those patterns again in the future. Traders that can incorporate these strategies into their own trading systems will find my scans to be their most valuable stock trading tool. While risk and uncertainty can never be eliminated, taking the time to become familiar with the results of a particular scan will usually reduce both.

Keep in mind that each one of these scans will present you with numerous candidates for trading ideas. You must study the charts and see if a high probability trade can be made. In other words, **not every result is a high probability candidate.** You must remember all the money management lessons covered in this book. They represent the skeleton of this stock picking method. Study the following chapters carefully. It should be worth many times the price of this book.

I will try to put all the pieces of the puzzle together, as I explain each one of the scans. I will include case studies of actual executed trades to support all my theories. This may cause some redundancy, and I apologize for that in advance. However, I want to be as thorough as possible, so you can all benefit from the greatest trading tool I have in my arsenal.

Scan Symbol	Oz Scan Name
$BOTFSHR-N	Oz NYSE Bottom Fisher Scan
$SKYSCRP-N	Oz NYSE Sky Scraper Scan
$SUSPECT-N	Oz NYSE Usual Suspect Scan
$KNOCKDN-N	Oz NYSE Knock Down Scan
$10WEEKS-N	Oz NYSE 10 1/2 Weeks Scan
$9WEEKS-N	Oz NYSE 9 1/2 Weeks Scan
$NEWKID-N	Oz NYSE New Kid Scan
$PWRTRDR-N	Oz NYSE Power Trader Scan
$GAPER-N	Oz NYSE Gaper Scan
$BOTFSHR-Q	Oz Nasdaq NMS Bottom Fisher Scan
$SKYSCRP-Q	Oz Nasdaq NMS Sky Scraper Scan
$SUSPECT-Q	Oz Nasdaq NMS Usual Suspect Scan
$KNOCKDN-Q	Oz Nasdaq NMS Knock Down Scan
$10WEEKS-Q	Oz Nasdaq NMS 10 1/2 Weeks Scan
$9WEEKS-Q	Oz Nasdaq NMS 9 1/2 Weeks Scan
$NEWKID-Q	Oz Nasdaq NMS New Kid Scan
$PWRTRDR-Q	Oz Nasdaq NMS Power Trader Scan
$GAPER-Q	Oz Nasdaq NMS Gaper Scan

TAL Chain listing

The above image is a screen shot of the Oz Scanner. If you want to know how you can get this tool, please visit www.tonyoz.com for more information. I hope that this tool will be available for as low as $20.00 a month.

NOTE: The basic formulas for the scans used in the following chapters were published in the books, *Stock Trading Wizard* and *The Stock Trader*. Due to copyright laws, we couldn't publish the formulas in this book. In the following chapters, I will tell you exactly what the scans are looking for, and more importantly, how to trade the stocks that show up on the different scans. It is important to tell you that I make minor adjustments as market conditions change. However, the basics of the formulas and the way to trade stocks that show up on the scan always stay the same.

135

CHAPTER **13**

Real-Time Scans - The Usual Suspects

The Usual Suspects
$SUSPECT-N and $SUSPECT-Q

One of the first successful trading strategies I developed was for stocks that traded higher in price on higher relative volume. It all started in 1994 when I was subscribing to the *Investors' Business Daily*. What I liked most about the paper was that it had tables, which featured stocks that were moving in price on higher than average volume. I would study each one of the stocks in great detail. I was looking for stocks that just broke out of a base.

Unfortunately, most of the stocks that broke out of a base already made a significant advance in price yesterday and would gap up the following day. However, many of them would still move higher the second day. On the third day, it would be time to take some profits off the table, because the stock would often gap up and sell off. Consequently, I realized that the *lucky* traders entered the stock on the **first** day it made its movement. The *smart* traders entered the stock on the **second** day, and the *bag-holders* entered the stock on the **third** day.

Since I remembered that a wise man once said, "I'd rather be lucky than smart," I knew that I had to discover a way to find these stocks on the first day of their move. Consequently, I developed the Usual Suspects Scan. This scan filters the entire market searching for stocks that are moving up and are on pace to trade higher than their average daily volume. I use this scan to see which stocks are moving. I try to detect the stocks early enough in the day. The ultimate candidate is a stock that breaks out after consolidation on relatively high volume. The following examples illustrate how I use the Usual Suspects Scan in my trading.

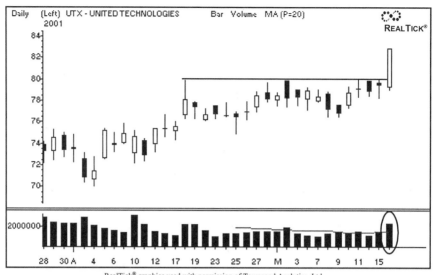

RealTick® graphics used with permission of Townsend Analytics, Ltd.

UTX showed up on my scan when it was trading at 79.80 and was on pace to trade higher than average volume. What I liked about this setup was that the stock has consolidated for four weeks and was finally breaking out through resistance. This is the first day of the move.

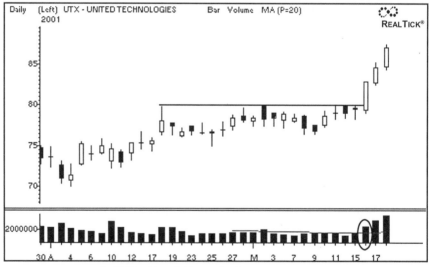

RealTick® graphics used with permission of Townsend Analytics, Ltd.

Over the next two days, UTX went up to 87.50. If I wasn't running an intraday scan, I would have never been able to find UTX on the first day of its move.

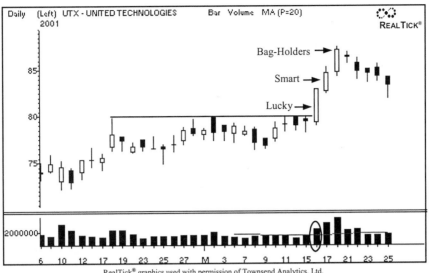

Daily (Left) UTX - UNITED TECHNOLOGIES   Bar Volume MA (P=20)

REALTICK®

RealTick® graphics used with permission of Townsend Analytics, Ltd.

This case study of UTX shows why this scan is so effective. The only way I could be one of the lucky ones to buy UTX was to discover it on the first day it made its move. Otherwise, I could find it by running an overnight scan. This would enable me to enter the stock when the smart traders entered it. The exit would normally be done on the third or fourth day. The above chart shows my three-day theory to perfection as the ones who bought the stock on the third day are now holding the bag.

One of the problems of waiting for day-two before entering the stock, (if you did not discover it on day-one), is that it is almost impossible to find an acceptable support level to place a stop loss. If we look at the above example again, the support level is the actual breakout point. However, UTX closed about three points higher than the breakout price level. If I were to buy the stock the next day at 83, I would need to have a price target of at least 92.75 to get a 3.00 reward/risk ratio as seen in the calculator.

TONY OZ Stock Market Calculator   Trading Plan

Entry Price	83	Reward/Risk Ratio 3.00
Target Price	92.75	Potential Profit 2925.00
Stop Loss	79.75	Potential Loss 975.00
Position Size	300	

Calculate

139

The risk of three points would have been too great, because I wouldn't have expected 92.75 to be a realistic price target. Consequently, I would have missed this trade completely have I not entered it with the lucky ones. Let's look at some other case studies for this scan.

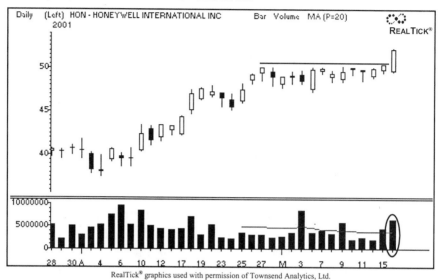

RealTick® graphics used with permission of Townsend Analytics, Ltd.

HON showed up on my scan when it was trading at 50 and was on pace to trade higher than average volume. What I liked about this setup was that the stock has consolidated for three weeks and was finally breaking out through resistance. Again, this is the first day of the move.

HON trades up to 54 over the next three trading days. If you bought the stock on day one, it would be smart to place a stop loss below the low of day-two and adjust the stop every day from that point forward. This would have kept you in the trade all the way to day four.

The previous example is very common and very realistic to what you could expect in terms of returns. If you were to buy the stock at 50 and sell it at 53.50, you would have captured a 7% return in three days. This falls right into the expectation levels for swing trading. A realistic goal for swing trading is 5%-15% returns in two to ten days per <u>successful</u> trade, (not your entire account!)

The Usual Suspects Scan can also be used to find stocks that are making a bottom. IP showed up on my scan when it was trading at 26.75 and was on pace to trade higher than average volume. What I liked about this setup was that the stock had come down in price for a while and was very active. This showed me that there was interest in the stock. As you can see, the low of the previous day was not taken out. The stock found great interest and traded up to 29.75.

RealTick® graphics used with permission of Townsend Analytics, Ltd.

141

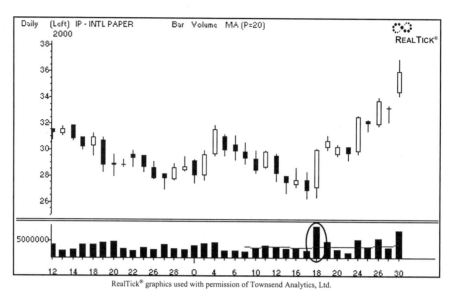

IP trades up to 37 over the next eight trading days. The big volume day was a good signal for a potential bottom for the stock. The 38% return in eight trading days was a huge bonus. The fact that the price pullbacks took place on low relative volume could have kept you in the trade through day-eight. However, if you only caught the price movement in day one, you could have still made 11% that day.

This case study is one of my favorites, because the setup is not as obvious as a breakout setup; yet, it provides you with unique opportunity to make extraordinary gains. The following strategy illustrates how I trade similar scenarios.

Reversal Day Trading Strategy

Stocks that have been trending downward for a while or even markets that have traded downward for a while are bound to make a bottom sooner or later. What I look for is a heavy volume day. I want the stock to be selling off from the opening bell and form a bottom. My entry point is crucial for the trade to be successful. The following example illustrates a classic potential reversal day.

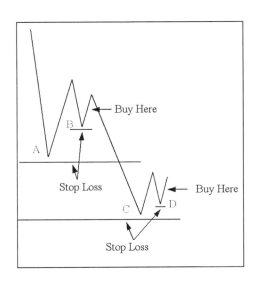

The stock in the above chart is selling off from the opening bell and forms a bottom at point A (normally around 20-45 minutes from the opening bell). The stock then rallies. I will look to see where that rally tops and follow the pullback very closely. Assuming that the pullback has bottomed at point B and the stock is beginning to tick up again, I will look to enter a long position at that point. Stop loss placement depending on the size of the trade and your comfort level can be placed either under point B or point A. If those levels are violated, you must get out of the trade! Then, look for the formation of the bottom at point C. Watch the rally very carefully. See if the pullback from that rally does not take out the low prices at point C. If it doesn't and the stock is trading higher from point D, then you can buy it! Place your stop loss under point C or D depending on your risk tolerance.

Often, if the stock held either bottom A or B, it will trade higher and take out the high of the day. The question many professionals ask me is why don't I wait until the stock takes out the high of the day and enter it then. My answer is that an entry at point B or D would be where the reward to risk is absolutely the greatest. An entry point over the mornings high can spell shaky position.

For instance, if I bought the stock once it took out the morning high, and the stock traced back 50% of the upswing, I might be shaken out of my position. However, if I bought the stock at point B or D, I can give it more wiggle room. Let's look at the following two examples of market bottoms on the Nasdaq to illustrate my philosophy.

143

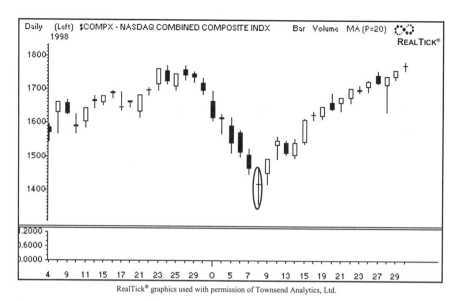

RealTick® graphics used with permission of Townsend Analytics, Ltd.

The above chart covers one of the most memorable days in my trading career, October 8th 1998, in which I utilized the reversal day strategy to perfection. However, I want to point out why using my strategy in this case would have given you the best possible entry and more likely keep you in the trade longer.

The low of the day on the Nasdaq was 1357. The high of the day was 1462. If you used the reversal day strategy, you would have been long at or around 1372. Your stop loss would have been placed at 1330 or so. If you were to buy it once it traded higher than 1465 and placed a stop loss at 1330, your risk would have been 135 points, which is 9.2% on the index. That is a big risk to take on the entire index. Even if you were willing to take that trade, it would have been very possible to be shaken out two days later (the black candle). However, using the reversal day strategy would have kept you in the trade because the entry was excellent.

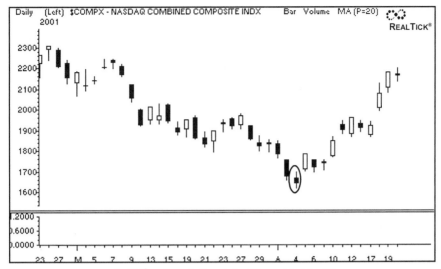

RealTick® graphics used with permission of Townsend Analytics, Ltd.

Another memorable day was April 3rd 2001. I had issued a reversal day strategy alert in my free monthly newsletter on the prior day. The low of the day was 1619, and the high of the day was 1698. If you followed the strategy, you would have entered the trade at about 1635. The following day, the index gapped up to 1709 and ran to 1785. If you entered the trade on the following day, you would have probably been stopped out the day after that. Regardless of where you entered the trade, you would have been down on your position. However, if you entered the trade on April 3rd, you would have most likely been able to sit in the trade.

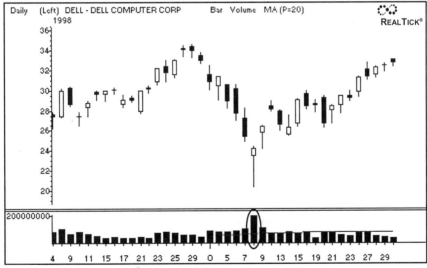

RealTick® graphics used with permission of Townsend Analytics, Ltd.

Here is one of the stocks I bought on October 8th 1998. DELL had a low of 20.38 and a high of 24.38. I used the reversal day strategy and bought the stock at 21.00. The next morning the stock opened at 25.69. I was up 21% on the trade. The stock then went down to 24.25. It then rallied and closed at 26.41. If I were to buy the stock at the open, I would have been stopped out. If I were to buy it once it took out the morning high on the second day, I would have paid 25.80 for it. Again, you can see how my "untraditional" way of doing things allowed me to have a great entry.

Stock Trading Math 101: Good Entry = Easier Trade

This scan is extremely powerful, but it has many flaws that you must be aware of. The first one is that you will get many results that you would have to filter through on a daily basis. Many of the results will not be high probability set-ups. I have added additional filters to this scan, which I will cover later on. However, I want to feature some of the common mistakes you could potentially make.

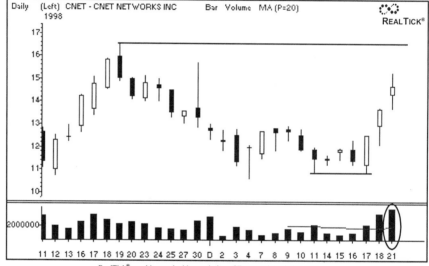

RealTick® graphics used with permission of Townsend Analytics, Ltd.

One of the most common errors that one can make is to enter a stock that has already started its swing. CNET had bottomed at 10.88 and started to trade up. However, the volume criteria was not met on the first day of the move. The stock did meet the volume criteria on the second day, but was already up 18% from the previous day. I would have not entered a trade there simply because it wouldn't have answered to an acceptable reward/risk ratio. If you chose to take this trade you would have gotten away with it as the stock traded up to 15.25. However, many traders would make the mistake of entering the stock on the third day because of the volume spike. They would anticipate that the stock would test the highs at 16.50.

146

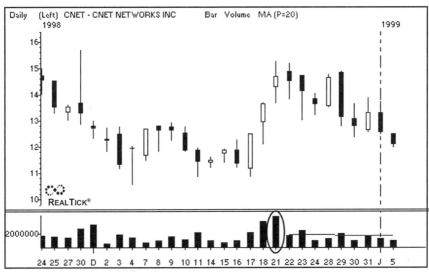

RealTick® graphics used with permission of Townsend Analytics, Ltd.

As you can see, CNET went down to 12.00 over the next two weeks. If you bought the stock on the volume spike day, you would have probably lost money. **It is important to understand that a volume spike on an up day isn't necessarily a buy signal.** You must take into consideration the move the stock has already made and remember that more often than not, you should let it go if you missed it.

I named this scan The Usual Suspects, because it looks for the same criteria I was getting out of The IBD's volume tables. When I used to study the stocks in the tables, my wife would often ask me, "Tony, what are you doing?" My answer would be, "I am just looking at the usual suspects."

14

Real-Time Scans - Knock Down

$KNOCKDN-N and $KNOCKDN-Q

The Knock Down Scan is very similar to the Usual Suspects Scan. This scan filters the entire market searching for stocks that are moving down and are on pace to trade higher than their average daily volume. I use this scan to see which stocks are moving. I try to detect the stocks early enough in the day. The ultimate candidate is a stock that breaks down after consolidation on relatively high volume. The following examples illustrate how I use the Usual Suspects Scan in my trading.

RealTick® graphics used with permission of Townsend Analytics, Ltd.

AA showed up on my Knock Down Scan when it was trading at 32.43 and was on pace to trade higher than average volume. What I liked about this setup was that the stock has consolidated for five weeks and was finally breaking down through support. This is the first day of the move. The only thing that bothered me about this short sell setup was the fact that AA was able to get back into the channel and close there. However, the increase in volume and the fact that AA has been making lower highs and lower lows inside the channel told me that sellers were somewhat more aggressive on this stock. Let's see what happened next.

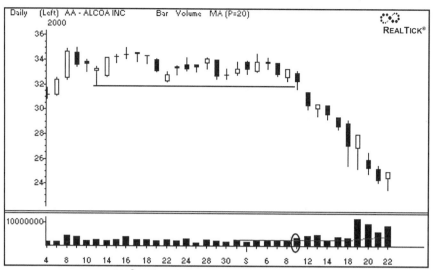

RealTick® graphics used with permission of Townsend Analytics, Ltd.

AA trades down to 23.50 over the next nine trading days. Please note that AA did not take out the high it made on the previous day on any of the following trading days. If you sold the stock short on day one and placed a stop loss above the high of the previous day, you would have been able to stay in the trade through day-nine. This should have resulted in a profit of 8.93 (27%).

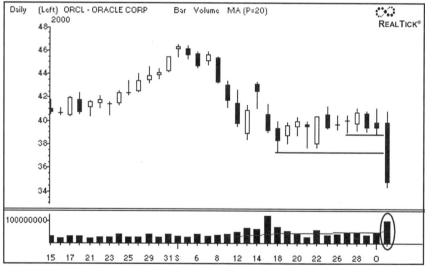

RealTick® graphics used with permission of Townsend Analytics, Ltd.

ORCL showed up on my Knock Down Scan when it was trading at 39.70 and was on pace to trade higher than average volume. The stock took out the support levels established on the previous four trading days. It then took out the major support level established two weeks ago. This was a great short setup.

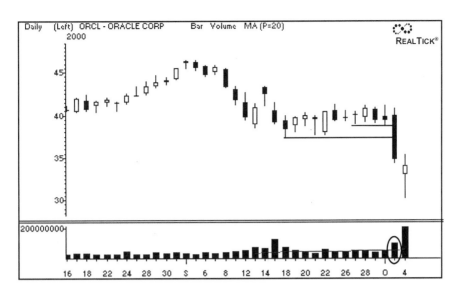

ORCL trades down to 30.25 the next day. If you sold the stock short around 38.50, you could have captured about 7-8 points (18%-20%) in two days. You could have used the reversal day strategy featured in the previous chapter to both cover your short and enter a possible long position.

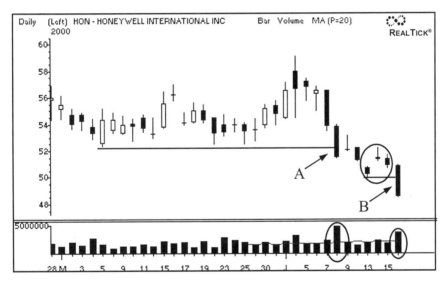

This case study is somewhat special, because we used HON in the last chapter to demonstrate a long position. This time we will use it to demonstrate a short position. HON showed up on my Knock Down Scan when it was trading at 49 (Point B), and it was on pace to trade higher than average volume. It would have also shown on my scan at Point A, but I took a day off that day. At point A, the stock broke through major support levels. What was showing tremendous weakness for the stock was the rally attempt that I circled on the chart. Every closing price was lower than the open. Once it showed up on my scan at 49 (Point B), I took a short position.

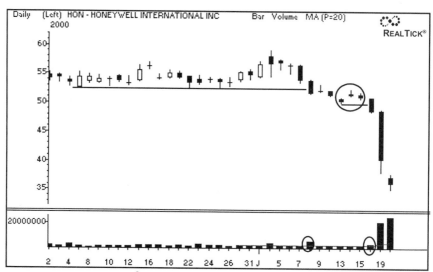

RealTick® graphics used with permission of Townsend Analytics, Ltd.

HON trades down to 35 over the next two days. If you sold the stock short around 49, you could have captured about 9-14 points (18%-28%) in two days. The key clue was that the rally attempt was extremely weak, which showed that sellers were in control. This was another huge winner generated by this scan. *This case study took place in 2000. It was a year before the GE - HON merger fallout.*

Just like the Usual Suspects Scan, this scan is also extremely powerful, but it has many flaws that you must be aware of. The major flaw is that you will get many results that you would have to filter through on a daily basis. Many of the results will not be high probability setups. Make sure that you look for the first day of the move and use high-probability low risk/high rewards setups.

I named this scan Knock Down, because it looks for stocks that are declining in price on high relative volume. These stocks are getting a serious punch from investors on Wall Street, so this is the reasoning behind the name.

15

Real-Time Scans - Power Trader

$PWRTRDR-N and $PWRTRDR-Q

The Power Trader Scan is very similar to the Usual Suspects Scan. This scan filters the entire market searching for stocks that are moving up and are on pace to trade higher than their average daily volume. The volume criteria of this scan is stricter than the Usual Suspects Scan. I also added stricter rules for the last price, gap open, and last trade as a percentage of the trading range. I use this scan to find stocks that are moving on relative high volume and are trading at the top of the day's trading range. I try to detect the stocks early enough in the trading day, but I will also look to see if any stocks from this scan are setting up at the end of the day. The ultimate candidate is a stock that is making its first day of a move on relatively high volume. The following examples illustrate how I use the Power Trader Scan in my trading.

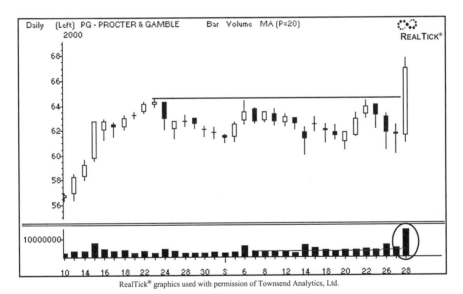

RealTick® graphics used with permission of Townsend Analytics, Ltd.

PG showed up on my Power Trader Scan when it was trading at 63.50 and was on pace to trade higher than average volume. What I liked about this setup was that the stock had consolidated for five weeks and was finally breaking out through resistance. This was the first day of the move.

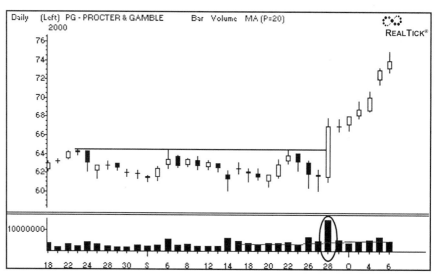

RealTick® graphics used with permission of Townsend Analytics, Ltd.

PG trades up to 74.88 over the next seven trading days. Please note that PG did not take out the high it made on the first day of the move, on day-two, or day-three. This is very common. If you bought the stock on day-one, it would be smart to place a stop loss below the low of day-two and adjust the stop with every day from that point forward. This would have kept you in the trade all the way to day seven.

Since this scan is very similar to the Usual Suspects Scan, you could use the same examples that were used in that chapter. We can also use this scan to find bottoms formed on high volume. The main difference between the two scans is that you will not get as many results on this scan as you would on the other one due to the stricter guidelines that this scan follows.

Stocks that show up on this scan at the end of the trading day have a 75% chance of making a higher high the following day. However, the higher high could be one cent higher, so do not hold these stocks overnight only because they have a 75% chance to make a higher high. You must remember that if you make this play ten times, and nine stocks went up 25 cents on average the following day, you could still lose money. Suppose that the tenth stock gapped down 15 points, it just wiped out the 2.25 extra profit you made on the previous nine trades by more than six times. You must use your discretion and only hold the stocks that look extremely promising based on their technical setups and reward/risk ratios.

I named this scan Power Trader, because it looks for stocks that are moving up in price on high relative volume and trade close to the high of the day. This shows a powerful move by the stock.

CHAPTER 16

Real-Time Scans - New Kid on the Block

$NEWKID-N and $NEWKID-Q

The New Kid on the Block Scan is very similar to the Power Trader Scan. This scan filters the entire market searching for stocks that are moving up and are on pace to trade higher than their average daily volume. The volume and price criteria of this scan is different than the Power Trader Scan. I use this scan to find stocks that are priced between 5-40 and are moving up on relative high volume. These stocks must be trading at the top 25% of the day's trading range.

The main difference between this scan and the Power Trader Scan is the minimum and maximum average daily volume criteria. This scan tries to find stocks that are relatively unknown and are finding interest from institutions or investors. I try to detect the stocks early enough in the trading day, but I will also look to see if any stocks from this scan are setting up at the end of the day. The ultimate candidate is a stock that is making its first day of a move on relatively high volume. The following examples illustrate how I use the New Kid on the Block Scan in my trading.

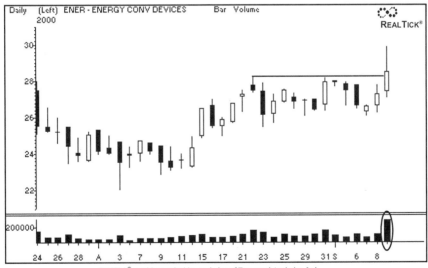

RealTick® graphics used with permission of Townsend Analytics, Ltd.

ENER showed up on my New Kid on the Block Scan when it was trading at 28 and was on pace to trade higher than average volume. What I liked about this setup was that the stock has consolidated for three weeks and was finally breaking out through resistance. This is the first day of the move. The way I trade stocks that come up on this scan and are breaking out to new highs is to start with a small position. More often than not, these stocks would sell off at the end of the day. At that point, I would look to add to my position. My trailing stop management utilizing this scan is to place a stop loss for 60%-80% of my position below the previous day's low. I would like to hang on to 20% of my position for as long as I can as long as the overall environment for the market, industry, and my stock remains bullish. You never know when you find the future Wall Street darling.

ENER sold off at the end of the day, but the volume spike would normally alert speculators who run overnight scans to this stock. More often than not, there is going to be some interest the following day.

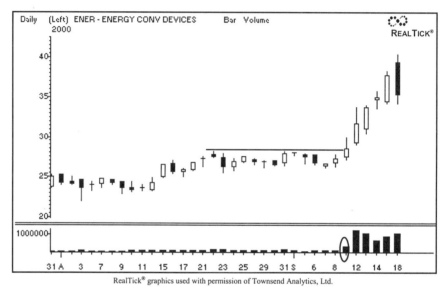

RealTick® graphics used with permission of Townsend Analytics, Ltd.

ENER traded up to 40. It was up about 43% since it came up on my New Kid on the Block Scan six days ago. As you can see in the chart, the stock did not take out the low made on the previous day, so if you were using my trailing stop methodology, you would have been able to stay in the trade through day-six. You can also see in the chart that the volume has increased drastically as Wall Street was discovering this "New Kid."

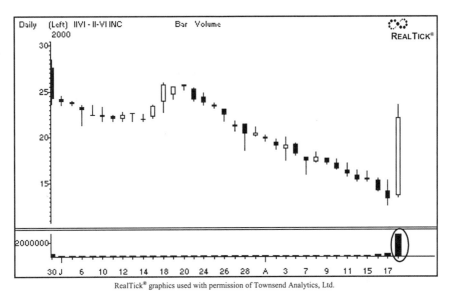

RealTick® graphics used with permission of Townsend Analytics, Ltd.

IVI showed up on my New Kid on the Block Scan when it was trading at 15.25 and was well on pace to trade higher than average volume. What I liked about this setup was that the stock has considerably declined in price. It was now going up on very high volume. This is the first day of the move. The stock trades up to 23.50. It is up 54% since we found it on our scan. This would be a good time to take profits on 80%-90% of the position and hold the rest.

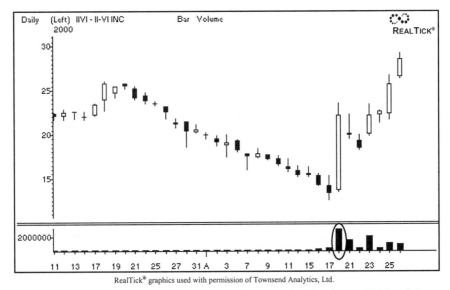

RealTick® graphics used with permission of Townsend Analytics, Ltd.

IVI pulls back over the next two days and gives back about 50% of the move it made from the low of the day. It then rallies back up and hits 29.75. This scan has enabled me to find IVI early enough in the day.

One of the hidden values that the New Kid on the Block Scan has is that it finds stocks that are moving on good news in real-time. If a stock releases good news and it trades with the news, this scan should pick it up if the stock meets all the other search criteria.

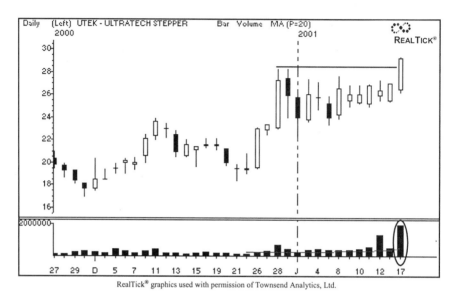

RealTick® graphics used with permission of Townsend Analytics, Ltd.

UTEK showed up on my New Kid on the Block Scan when it was trading at 28 and was on pace to trade higher than average volume. What I liked about this setup was that the stock has consolidated for more than two weeks and was breaking out through resistance. This is the first day of the move. Everything was just ripe for this stock to move higher. The volume was there, the market was supportive, and the time of year was right. This breakout occurred during the January Effect time period.

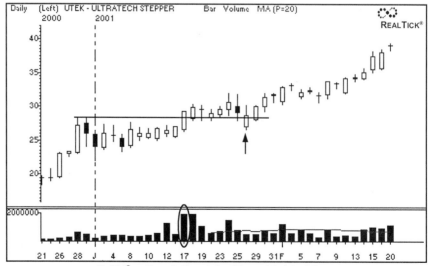

RealTick® graphics used with permission of Townsend Analytics, Ltd.

This was one of the toughest trades. I was shaken out numerous times, because the market makers were gapping the stock down on a daily basis. However, the stock would always trade back up. The day I lost my position was the day before the stock gapped down through the breakout price level (marked by the arrow). It was the first day that the stock closed lower than it opened and formed a black body candle.

I was able to trade UTEK successfully numerous times during its upswing. I would have never found this stock if it weren't for my New Kid on the Block Scan. What was truly amazing about this stock was that the market makers were trying to take it down before the open, so they could average a lower price for whomever they were buying the stock. However, the stock was very strong as you can see on the chart. There are many more white body candles than black ones.

I chose this example because it is not perfect. The support line was violated and the market makers were making this trade extremely challenging. However, I wanted you to see that I am not cherry-picking the case studies, and that I lose my positions many times. In spite of losing my position numerous times, I entered the stock again and turned a profit on it while not breaking any money management rules.

The following charts show additional stocks that showed up on this scan. The arrows will point to the day it showed up on the scan.

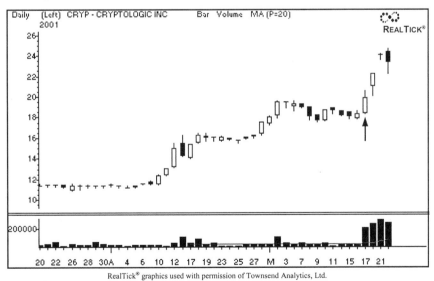

RealTick® graphics used with permission of Townsend Analytics, Ltd.

CRYP showed up on this scan after it consolidated for about two weeks. The powerful move on high volume was a great signal to enter a long position.

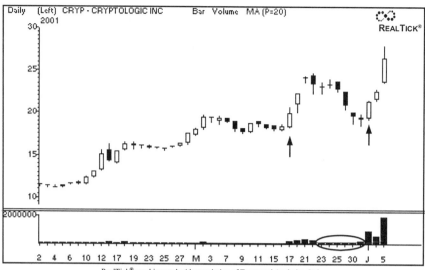

RealTick® graphics used with permission of Townsend Analytics, Ltd.

About two weeks after CRYP showed up on the scan, it showed up again. As you can see in the above chart, CRYP pulled back from the highs it made after the first time it showed up on the scan on relatively low volume. As soon as volume picked up again, the New Kid on the Block Scan was able to find the stock and alert me to it. The stock moved up sharply in price over the next three days.

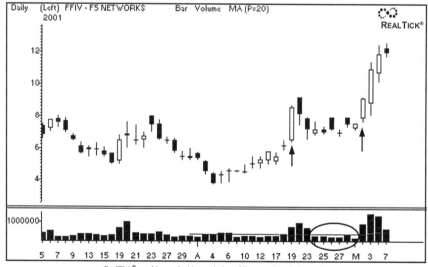

RealTick® graphics used with permission of Townsend Analytics, Ltd.

The above chart shows a similar pattern. FFIV showed up on the scan twice within two weeks. Just like CRYP, FFIV pulled back from the first top it made after the first time it showed up on the scan on low relative volume. The New Kid on the Block Scan was able to find FFIV on the day the volume picked up again and just before it made its explosive move up.

Stocks that show up on this scan may represent incredible opportunities. Almost all of Wall Street's darlings would have showed up on this scan before they became popular. Consequently, traders, investors, or even fund managers can use this scan to find stocks with new interest. However, you should all be aware of the problems this scan might represent you with.

The first thing you should be aware of is that if a chatroom or a message-board is pumping a thin stock, it would show up on this scan. Consequently, you must use extreme caution.

Next, if any market participant manipulates the stock by painting the tape, it would also show up on the scan. Although this practice is illegal, it could still happen. You must be careful.

Then, if a block trade takes place for a thinly traded stock, it may result that the stock would show up on the scan. You must make sure that the volume on your RealTick® intraday chart is active. To do so press the F4 key and check the box next to "show volume." Once you have volume on the intraday chart, you must make sure that the volume has been steady throughout the trading day.

Finally, this scan would also catch stocks that are moving on rumors. This could be dangerous if the rumors turned out to be false. To be on the safe side, you should take relative small positions in the stocks that show up on this scan.

All in all, this scan is extremely valuable in bull markets, at the end of a bear market, and during the January Effect. In one of the three stock-picking contests that I have won, 40% of all trades were generated by this scan.

I named this scan New Kid on the Block, because it searches for stocks that are not well known.

CHAPTER 17

Real-Time Scans - 10 ½ Weeks

$10WEEKS-N and $10WEEKS-Q

The 10 ½ Weeks Scan filters the entire market searching for stocks that are moving up and are making a new 53-day high on higher than average daily volume. Candidates from this scan can be for either a long or short position. If a stock is breaking out after consolidation it could be a candidate for a long position. If a stock has been going up for a while and gapped up, yet, it is trading lower than the opening price, it would be considered for a short position. Stocks which are making a 2-month high, 6-month high, or 52-week high on higher than average volume will also show up on this scan. The following examples illustrate how I use the 10 ½ Weeks Scan in my trading.

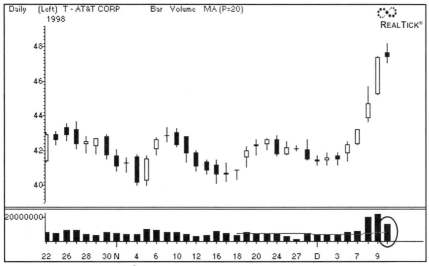

RealTick® graphics used with permission of Townsend Analytics, Ltd.

T showed up on my 10 ½ Week Scan when it was trading at 48 and was on pace to trade higher than average volume. The stock gapped up open and traded as high as 48.19. Then, sellers took over, and the stock traded through the opening price of 47.70. I was looking to enter a short position on the stock. My conservative price target for a short position on an up-trending stock in a bull market based on the corrective phase approach was 45.50. My entry price was 47.65 and my stop loss was placed at 48.31.

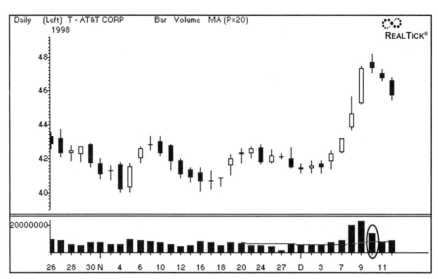

RealTick® graphics used with permission of Townsend Analytics, Ltd.

T trades down to 45.50 over the next two trading days and hits the price target right on the nose. This is an example of how I use the 10 ½ Weeks Scan to find potential short candidates.

The setups I use for long positions from this scan are basically identical to the UTX and HON in the Usual Suspects chapter, or PG in the Power Trader chapter.

I named this scan 10 ½ Weeks, because 53 trading days are approximately 10 ½ weeks.

18

Real-Time Scans - 9 ½ Weeks

$9WEEKS-N and $9WEEKS-Q

The 9 ½ Weeks Scan filters the entire market searching for stocks that are moving down and are making a new 47-day low on higher than average daily volume. Candidates from this scan can be for either a long or short position. If a stock is breaking down after consolidation it could be a candidate for a short position. If a stock has been going down for a while and gapped down, yet, it is trading higher than the opening price, it would be considered for a long position. Stocks that are making a 2-month low, 6-month low, or 52-week low on higher than average volume will also show up on this scan. The following examples illustrate how I use the 9 ½ Weeks Scan in my trading.

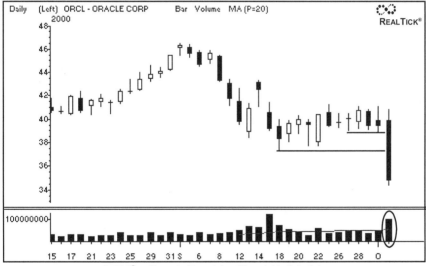

RealTick® graphics used with permission of Townsend Analytics, Ltd.

ORCL is an example of a short candidate based on the 9 ½ Weeks scan. It is just breaking through support levels (bear flag), on increasing trading volume.

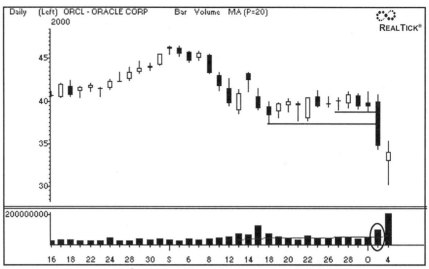

RealTick® graphics used with permission of Townsend Analytics, Ltd.

The following day, ORCL is a candidate for a long position, because it gapped down and traded back up over its opening price. Please note that I would use the reversal day strategy for potential long positions for stocks that have traded down for a while and are making a new 47-day low just as I illustrated in the chapter that covers the Knock Down Scan.

I named this scan 9½ Weeks, because 47 trading days are approximately 9½ weeks.

CHAPTER 19

Real-Time Scans - Gapper

$GAPER-N and $GAPER-Q

The Gapper Scan filters the entire market searching for stocks that gap open and are currently trading at a price that is higher than the opening price. These stocks must meet additional screening criteria such as minimum average daily volume and trading range. If a stock gaps up and is able to trade higher than the opening price, it is showing signs of strength. Most of the time, the gap open is a result of good news. The strategies behind this scan are somewhat tricky, so please pay close attention to the rules and logic behind this scan. The following examples illustrate how I use the Gapper Scan in my trading.

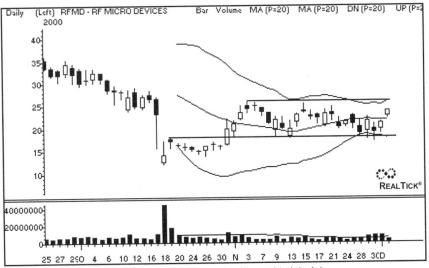

RealTick® graphics used with permission of Townsend Analytics, Ltd.

RFMD showed up on my Gapper Scan when it was trading at 23.00. It was trading higher than the opening price of 22.63. When I use the Gapper Scan, I take a close look at the stock and its normal trading pattern. Bollinger Bands are a very useful tool to see any deviation from the normal price action. What I liked about RFMD was the fact that the bands were close together. The stock has been trading in a channel between 18 and 26 for the last five weeks. If the stock was to breakout of the channel, it could very easily trade above the Upper Bollinger Band. Let's see what happened next.

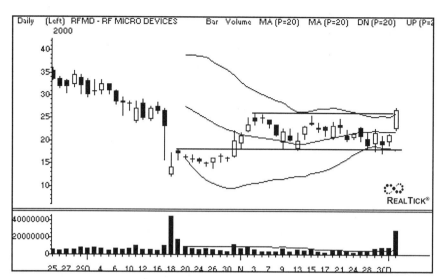

RFMD breaks out through the Upper Bollinger Band and the channel on high volume. It closes at 26.94. The strong volume and the fact that the stock was just at the bottom of its trading channel two days ago give us a strong clue to future price movement. *Please note, RFMD showed up on the Usual Suspects, Power Trader, and Gapper scans on the day of its breakout.*

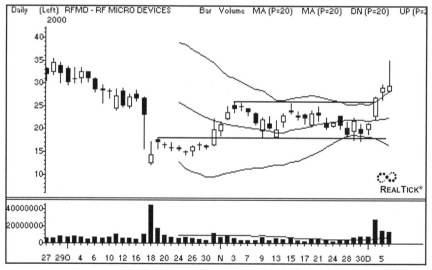

Over the next two days, RFMD trades up to 35.13. It is up 52% since it came up on my Gapper Scan. This is where you have to control *GREED*. The stock has made a big move in a short period of time. It would be wise to take profits. As you can see in the chart, the wise traders cashed in their profits, and the stock sold off. It closed at 29.50. This case study also shows the three-day methodology. The **lucky** ones found RFMD on the **first** day of its move. The **smart** ones entered the stock on the **second** day of its move. The **bag-holders** bought the stock at 32-35 on the **third** day of the move and are now looking to break even, because the stock closed at 29.50.

Let's look at another example on the same stock.

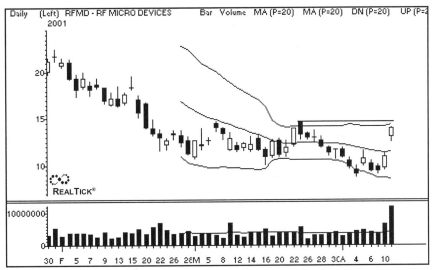

RealTick® graphics used with permission of Townsend Analytics, Ltd.

RFMD showed up on my Gapper Scan when it was trading at 13.50. It was trading higher than the opening price of 13.00. What I liked about RFMD was the fact that the low price the stock traded at last week was the 26-month low. The stock has been trading down for a while. The up day prior to the gap open was on high relative volume. Volume increased today as the stock moved towards resistance at 14.50 (the Upper Bollinger Band), and 14.75 (the previous high). My only concern was the tremendous overhead supply at the higher price levels. Consequently, I knew that the volume would have to remain strong in order to have a strong sustainable rally. Let's see what happened next.

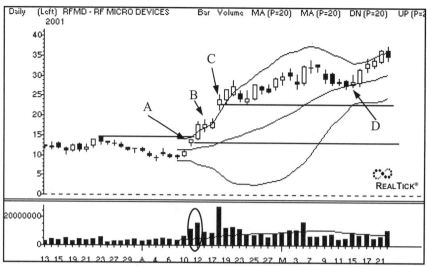

RealTick® graphics used with permission of Townsend Analytics, Ltd.

Point A shows the day the stock showed up on my Gapper Scan. The bottom horizontal line shows the gap-opening price, which I like to use as a stop loss level. The stock took out the resistance level out on the next trading day and consolidated for two days (Point B). Then, the stock gapped up again on strong earnings report (Point C), and traded above the Upper Bollinger Band for three days. The top horizontal line shows the gap-opening price, which we use as a trailing stop for this trade, or an initial stop loss if you entered the trade at Point C. The stock then traded above its 20-day MA but lower than the Upper Bollinger Band for the next three weeks. The 20-day MA caught up to the stock at Point D, and the stock traded back up to the Upper Bollinger band at 35-37. This would have been a good place to exit the trade.

To summarize this case study, I found RFMD at 13.50 by using the Gapper Scan. The stock went up to 37 (186%) over the following six weeks. The stock actually gapped-open twice and neither gap-opening prices were taken out. The pullback down to the 20-day MA was on low relative volume, and the bounce off the 20-day MA was on high relative volume. On the last day, the stock traded the highest volume over the last two days and closed below the opening price. This was a great signal to get out of the trade. Let's look at more examples.

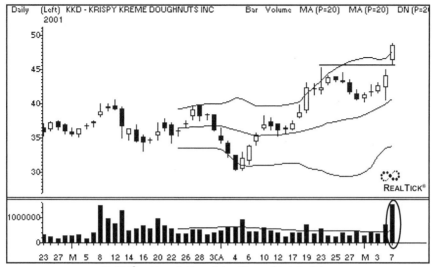

RealTick® graphics used with permission of Townsend Analytics, Ltd.

KKD showed up on my Gapper Scan when it was trading at 46.75. It was trading higher than the opening price of 46.22. What I did not liked about KKD was the fact that the Bollinger Bands were extremely expanded. I did like the high volume and breakout though. However, I knew I could not expect the stock to go vertical without some consolidation.

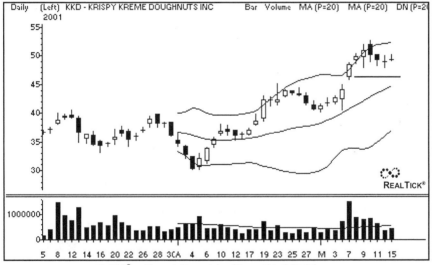

RealTick® graphics used with permission of Townsend Analytics, Ltd.

KKD did move higher, but the low the stock made the day after the gap-open was taken out on the following trading day. This would have made staying in the trade extremely difficult. The following day the stock gaped up and sold off. The next two days, the stock made lower highs and lower lows. It would have been a violation of money management rules to stay in this trade. However, position traders, who would have used the gap-opening price as a stop loss level, may have stayed in the trade while most of us wouldn't.

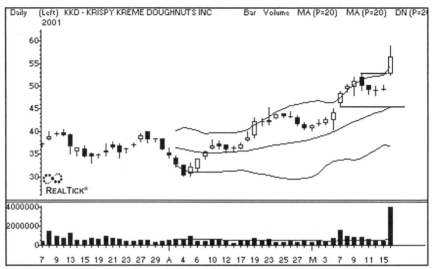

RealTick® graphics used with permission of Townsend Analytics, Ltd.

In a very similar manner to RFMD, KKD enjoyed the same fortune of good news and gapped up again. The stock traded up over resistance. Although it showed up on my Gapper Scan again, I did not trade it. The reason I did not trade it was that I had an opinion rather than watching the tape and the chart. I didn't feel that a doughnuts outfit was warranted the valuation The Street was giving KKD. I was not comfortable with it, so I passed on the trade.

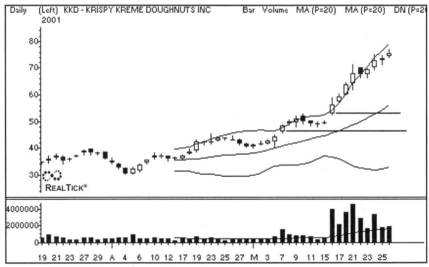

RealTick® graphics used with permission of Townsend Analytics, Ltd.

KKD traded straight up on high volume like a moon rocket. The shorts were getting killed on this stock. The low float, large relative short interest, and positive news were the major contributing factors for the sharp upswing in price. After we study the following example, I will explain these factors in greater detail.

RATL showed up on my Gapper Scan when it was trading at 102. It was trading higher than the opening price of 100. What I did not liked about RATL was the fact that the Bollinger Bands were extremely expanded. I did like the high volume and breakout, though. However, the Nasdaq was showing great weakness. Let's see what happened next.

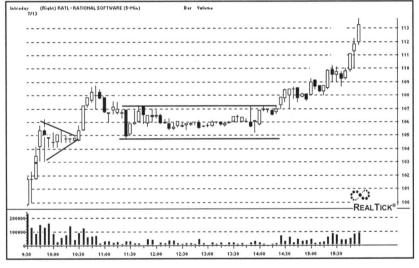

The above intraday chart shows the price action for RATL. The stock ran out of the gate and topped at 106.25 about twenty minutes after the open. It then formed a continuation pattern (symmetrical triangle) over the next forty minutes. Next, the stock broke out again and traded as high as 108.75. The stock topped out around 10:50 AM and declined back to 104.87. The stock entered the typical flat two and a half hour time period and traded between 105-107. I entered the stock in that channel and placed a stop loss at 104.62. I liked the strength the stock was showing, and I knew that the key number to know if I was right or wrong was the low at 104.87. The fact that the low price was not taken out throughout the flat time period was an encouraging sign. The stock later in the day broke out and was trading at 113. I was faced with a big dilemma. Should I sell or should I hold? I decided to sell and here is why:

RealTick® graphics used with permission of Townsend Analytics, Ltd.

The above chart has been adjusted for a 2 for 1 stock split. As you can see, RATL was trading between the 20-day MA and the Upper Bollinger Band for a while. I felt that the last price move was not very typical for the stock. Although it closed at the high of the day, I was skeptical about the probability of further price appreciation the following day. I wasn't skeptical only because RATL was extended over its Upper Bollinger Band, but also because the Nasdaq penetrated through its Upper Bollinger Band as well. I felt that the odds for a pullback were very high at this point.

My analysis proved to be right on the money. As you can see on the above chart, RATL gapped down and traded lower. Over the following two weeks, the stock went down below 90 (45 post split). My exit at 111.75 was the right thing to do in this case. This case study integrates another important factor for not only the Gapper Scan, but also for all trades we make. We must take into account the overall market

The Gapper Scan can be very effective if used properly. However it requires tremendous skill and experience level. The purpose behind this scan is to find stocks that are showing strength and momentum for a potential position trade following major news events. In order to use this scan and the strategies behind it successfully, you must master the following guidelines:

Prior to entering the stock, you must read the news carefully. Stay away from stocks that announce mergers. There is limited upside potential after the news is released. Try to focus on stocks that are surprising the Street with bullish forecasts especially if the Street was anticipating bearish news.

It is important to pay attention to both the float of a stock and the short interest it has, especially for stocks that have been trading down for a while. More often than not, stocks that release positive news and have large short interest and low float will explode in price. You can find both short interest and float on the web. If you use RealTick®, you can select "favorites" then "web browser" then choose one of the research tools there to find more information about the company.

Learn how to use Bollinger Bands effectively. Pay close attention and see if the Bands were contracting or expanding prior to the gap. Make sure that you determine if the stock has traded up in anticipation of the news, or if the news was a total surprise. And don't forget to analyze the market and determine if it can support your trade.

I named this scan Gapper, because it looks for stocks that had a gap open.

CHAPTER 20

Real-Time Scans - Bottom Fisher

$BOTFSHR-N and $BOTFSHR-Q

The Bottom Fisher Scan filters the entire market searching for stocks that have traded down for at least three consecutive trading sessions and are currently trading higher and signaling that a potential short-term bottom might have been formed. These stocks must meet additional screening criteria such as minimum average daily volume and trading range. Based on swing trading methodology, this scan is the bread and butter of my trading. The logic behind this scan is that it finds stocks that are trying to turn around after at least three consecutive down days. It represents me with higher reward to risk ratio than any other scan I use, because of the money management system I incorporated into this setup. The following examples illustrate how I use the Bottom Fisher Scan in my trading.

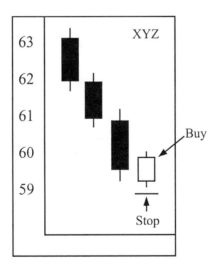

The basic setup is featured in the above illustration. It can be used for a stock that is in an uptrend or downtrend. The trigger event for an entry is for the stock to be up from yesterday's close. As long as a stop loss below today's low is an acceptable risk while trying to capture the price target reward, you can enter the trade. Otherwise, you would have to use intraday support levels. I will include numerous examples and case studies for this setup, because I want you to have a complete understanding of how I trade this powerful setup.

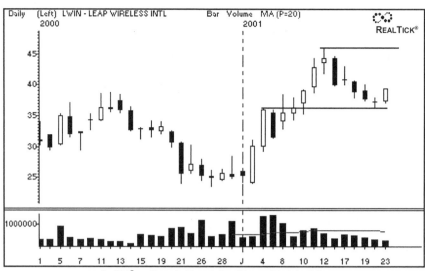

RealTick® graphics used with permission of Townsend Analytics, Ltd.

LWIN represents a classic swing trading setup. It showed up on my scan when it was trading at 39.10. The low of the day was 37.19. If I were to buy it, my stop loss would be placed 5 cents below 37. My price target would be the previous high minus 25 cents. The high was 46, so my price target would be 45.75. Let's plug these numbers into my calculator.

TONY OZ Stock Market Calculator	Trading Plan	
Entry Price	39.10	
Target Price	45.75	Reward/Risk Ratio 3.09
Stop Loss	36.95	Potential Profit 1995.00
Position Size	300	Potential Loss 645.00

Since the reward/risk ratio is greater than three, this would be an acceptable trade. I must mention that there is a significant difference between the traditional swing trading methodology and the methodology and money management I have developed for this scan. If you were to use my system, you would have bought the stock at 39.10. Let's use this case study to compare my swing trading system with the traditional swing trading system.

RealTick® graphics used with permission of Townsend Analytics, Ltd.

At the end of day, LWIN closed at 41.00, but it traded as high as 41.25. The traditional swing trading methodology would be to buy LWIN the following day should it trade higher than 41.50. A stop loss should be placed 25 cents below the 37.19 low. The price target would still be 45.75. Let's plug these numbers into my calculator.

TONY OZ Stock Market Calculator

Trading Plan

Entry Price	41.51	
Target Price	45.75	
Stop Loss	36.94	
Position Size	300	

Reward/Risk Ratio	0.93
Potential Profit	1272.00
Potential Loss	1371.00

The reward to risk ratio in this case is less than one. There would be no way that I could enter this trade according to my money management system. Yet, if you subscribe to swing trading advisory newsletters, you would see them recommend such trades frequently. Let's see what happened next.

RealTick® graphics used with permission of Townsend Analytics, Ltd.

LWIN goes up to 45.38 the very next day. It then sells off and trades below 40. If I were using my trailing stop system, I would have sold the stock north of 45 and pocket almost six points in profit. If I were to use the traditional swing trading system and buy the stock on the second day, I would most likely be in it at 42.20, and depending on the newsletter that I followed, I could have realistically made two points or even lost money.

The difference between my approach and the traditional approach is crystal clear. There is no need to wait until the next trading day to enter a position if you are running the Bottom Fisher Scan. Another beauty of this scan is that it could be used also at the end of the day. In fact, most swing trading advisory services use the basics of this scan to find trades for the next morning. However, you should definitely see the benefits of using this scan in real-time. Now that you understand the main difference between my approach and the traditional approach, we can study the following examples.

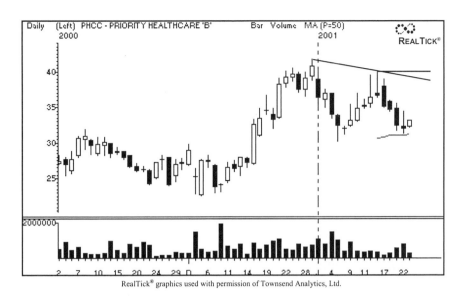

RealTick® graphics used with permission of Townsend Analytics, Ltd.

PHCC showed up on my Bottom Fisher Scan when it was trading at 33.12. The stock was up for the first time after four consecutive down days. The resistance level for the stock is the previous top at 39.80 or the downtrend line through the previous two tops at 38.50. The low of the day was 32.25. The first thing I need to do is see if I can have a trading plan that answers to my money management system.

TONY OZ Stock Market Calculator	Trading Plan	
Entry Price	33.12	
	Reward/Risk Ratio	4.38
Target Price	38.25	
	Potential Profit	1539.00
Stop Loss	31.95	
	Potential Loss	351.00
Position Size	300	

Since the reward/risk ratio was greater than three, I decided to enter the trade. The stop loss was placed at 31.95. Since 32 is a whole number, I gave the trade an extra five cents than the normal 25 cents from the low of the day stop. Let's follow this trade in more detail.

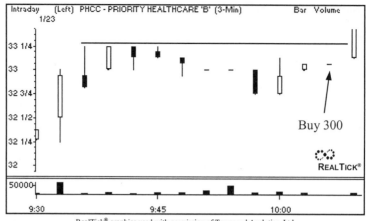

RealTick® graphics used with permission of Townsend Analytics, Ltd.

The above chart shows the intraday action on PHCC. The stock ran up from 32 to 33.25 where it topped. The stock then consolidated between 32.75 and 33.25. I bought 300 shares at 33.12. The stock then broke out.

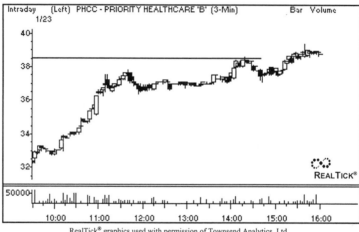

RealTick® graphics used with permission of Townsend Analytics, Ltd.

The stock was very strong and traded up to my 38.25 price target. I sold my 300 shares at 38.25 for a net profit of $1,517.11.

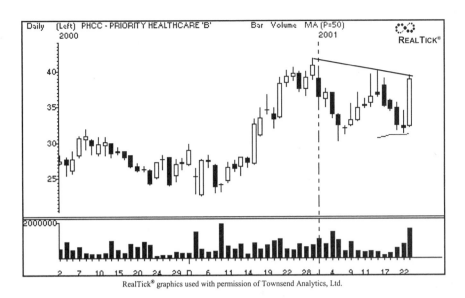

RealTick® graphics used with permission of Townsend Analytics, Ltd.

Here is what the chart looked like at the end of the trading day. The price target was met in one day. However, if I were not using the Bottom Fisher Real-Time Scan, I would have never been able to make this trade. If I were using the end of day data, I would have missed this trade.

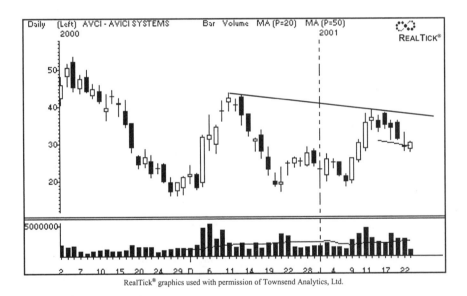

RealTick® graphics used with permission of Townsend Analytics, Ltd.

AVCI showed up on my Bottom Fisher Scan when it was trading at 30.25. The stock was up for the first time after three consecutive down days. The resistance level for the stock is the previous top at 39.12 or the downtrend line through the previous two tops at 37.80. The low of the day was 27.75. The first thing I need to do is see if I can have a trading plan that answers to my money management system.

TONY OZ	Stock Market Calculator	Trading Plan	

Entry Price	30.25	Reward/Risk Ratio	2.65
Target Price	37.55	Potential Profit	2190.00
Stop Loss	27.50	Potential Loss	825.00
Position Size	300		

As you can see, I couldn't take the trade, because the reward/risk ratio was smaller than three. Consequently, I needed to find intraday support levels to place my stop under.

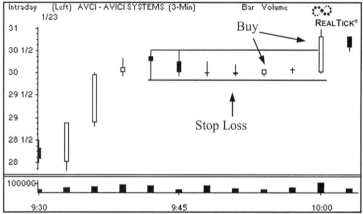

RealTick® graphics used with permission of Townsend Analytics, Ltd.

The above chart shows the intraday action on AVCI. The stock ran up from 27.75 to 30.50 where it topped. The stock then consolidated between 29.87 and 30.37. I felt that if the stock would trade down through 29.87 it would be a bearish signal, and if it traded up through 30.50 it would be a bullish signal. I decided to buy half a position at 30.25. I placed a stop loss at 29.67. Should the stock trade higher than 30.50, I would complete my position and trail a stop loss.

Trading Plan

Entry Price	30.25
Target Price	37.55
Stop Loss	29.67
Position Size	300

Reward/Risk Ratio	12.59
Potential Profit	2190.00
Potential Loss	174.00

This plan provided me with reward/risk ratio that was greater than 12. It was my kind of risk management. The stock broke out, and I completed my position at 30.67. My average cost was 30.46 and the reward/risk ratio was now 8.97. Let's see what happened next.

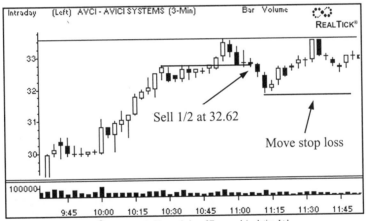

RealTick® graphics used with permission of Townsend Analytics, Ltd.

AVCI trades up to 33.50. I sold ½ of my position at 32.62 and locked in 2.16 (7%) in profits. The stock was up 5.75 from the low to the high. I still liked the strength in the stock, so I decided to watch the pullback carefully. I was going to use the low of that pullback as my stop loss for the remainder of my position.

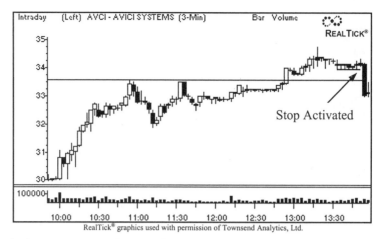

RealTick® graphics used with permission of Townsend Analytics, Ltd.

AVCI traded up to 35. It then pulled back to 34. The stock was bouncing off 34 for 20 minutes. I moved my stop loss to 33.87. I felt that if 34 was to be taken out, the stock could fall down hard. I sold the remainder of my position at 33.87. I captured a profit 3.41 (11%) on this part of the position. I bet you want to know what happened next.

RealTick® graphics used with permission of Townsend Analytics, Ltd.

AVCI traded up to 38.88 and met the price target. The reason I did not enter the trade again was that I felt the risk was not worth the reward since the stock was up so much. At this point, I must confess that all three trades illustrated above took place on the **same day**. In addition, I had open positions in both OPWV and CSCO. I definitely had my plate full, but I was not trading outside of my comfort level. However, I managed each one of my trades according to its plan.

The other interesting thing is that all three trades that came from the Bottom Fisher Scan were huge winners that day. It isn't always so. Moreover, I would have never found these stocks if it wasn't for the Real-Time Bottom

Fisher Scan, and the money I made that day paid for the scanner for the next 25 years. Let's look at more examples.

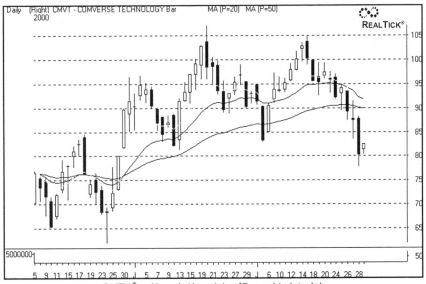

RealTick® graphics used with permission of Townsend Analytics, Ltd.

CMVT showed up on the Bottom Fisher Scan when it was trading at 82.50. Notice the sharp pullback the stock had from a double top formation at 105. I felt that the stock could rally back up to the high 80's or low 90's.

RealTick® graphics used with permission of Townsend Analytics, Ltd.

The above chart shows the intraday price action for CMVT. The arrow shows the point which the stock showed up on the scan. Notice that the stock rallied from a double bottom formation. This was a good high reward low risk setup. The stop is placed below the low of the day. The bottom range of the price target is met within three hours.

RealTick® graphics used with permission of Townsend Analytics, Ltd.

PMCS showed up on the Bottom Fisher Scan when it was trading at 182. Notice the sharp pullback the stock had from 230. I felt that the stock could rally back up to the 190's.

RealTick® graphics used with permission of Townsend Analytics, Ltd.

The above chart shows the intraday price action for PMCS. The arrow shows the point which the stock showed up on the scan. Notice that the stock pulled back down and tested the low of the day, but it never traded lower. Consequently, a stop loss below the low of the day would not have triggered. Again, the price target was met within three hours.

RealTick® graphics used with permission of Townsend Analytics, Ltd.

FLEX showed up on the Bottom Fisher Scan when it was trading at 71. What I liked about this setup is that the stock has pulled back sharply and was holding the 50-day MA. I felt that the stock could rally back up to the high 70's.

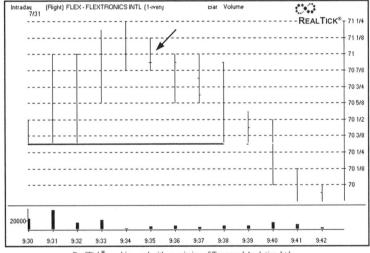

RealTick® graphics used with permission of Townsend Analytics, Ltd.

The above chart shows the intraday price action for FLEX. The arrow shows the point in which the stock showed up on the scan. A stop loss is placed below the morning low at 70.12. The stop is triggered moments later. Let's see what happened after.

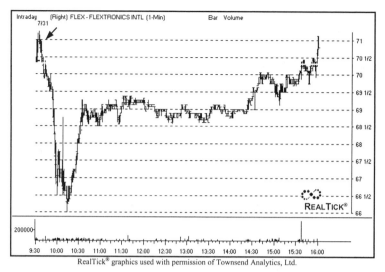

Once the stock took out the low of the day it sold off sharply. Although it did rally at the end of the day, I could have suffered a substantial loss on this trade.

What I like about this example the most is that the initial setup was one of high probability. The stock seemed to find support at the 50-day MA. It moved up at first only to sell off sharply moments later. This is why stop loss placement is crucial no matter how good the setup looks.

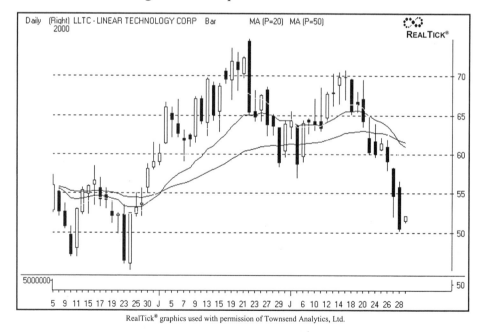

LLTC showed up on the Bottom Fisher Scan when it was trading at 52.40. Notice the sharp pullback the stock had from 70. I felt that the stock could rally back up to the mid 50's.

RealTick® graphics used with permission of Townsend Analytics, Ltd.

The above chart shows the intraday price action for LLTC. The arrow shows the point which the stock showed up on the scan. As you can see, the stock pulled back down and tested the low of the day. The stock penetrated through and traded lower by 12 cents. Consequently, a stop loss below the low of the day could have been triggered. Again, the price target was met within three hours.

I really like this example, because it shows how close calls are a part of every-day trading. If I had a stop loss that was greater than 15 cents below the low of the day, I could have made five points in profit. If my stop loss was be-tween 1-12 cents below the low of the day, I would have lost one point.

The Bottom Fisher Scan and the Sky Scraper Scan are simple to learn and im-plement. There are months that more than 30% of the setups I trade are gener-ated by those two scans. If you can master the Bottom Fisher and the Sky Scraper scans, you can become a successful trader even if you don't utilize any other strategy.

I named this scan Bottom Fisher, because it looks for stocks that might have formed a short-term bottom.

191

21

Real-Time Scans - Sky Scraper

$SKYSCRP-N and $SKYSCRP-Q

The Sky Scraper Scan filters the entire market searching for stocks that have traded up for at least three consecutive trading sessions and are currently trading lower and signaling that a potential short-term top might have been formed. These stocks must meet additional screening criteria such as minimum average daily volume and trading range. The logic behind this scan is that it finds stocks that are trying to turn around after at least three consecutive up days. Just like the Bottom fisher Scan, this scan represents me with higher reward to risk ratio than any other scan I use, because of the money management system I incorporated into this setup. The following examples illustrate how I use the Sky Scraper Scan in my trading.

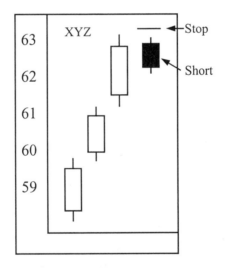

The basic setup is featured in the above illustration. It can be for a stock that is in an uptrend or downtrend. The trigger event for an entry is for the stock to be down from yesterday's close. As long as a stop loss above today's high is an acceptable risk while trying to capture the price target reward, you can enter the trade. Otherwise, you would have to use intraday resistance levels. I will include numerous examples and case studies for this setup, because I want you to have a complete understanding of how I trade this powerful setup.

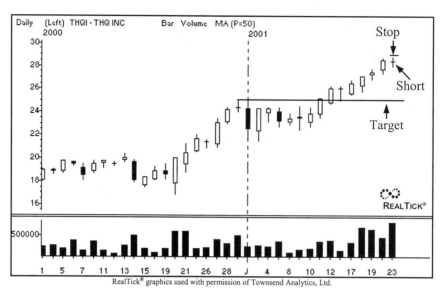

THQI showed up on the Sky Scraper Scan when it was trading at 28.20. The stock had enjoyed a nice run, and I felt that it could go down to test the previous highs at 24.80 (horizontal line). The plan was to short the stock at 28.20 and place a stop loss at 28.95 (0.20 over the high of the day). The reward to risk in this case is 4.5. Let's see what happened next.

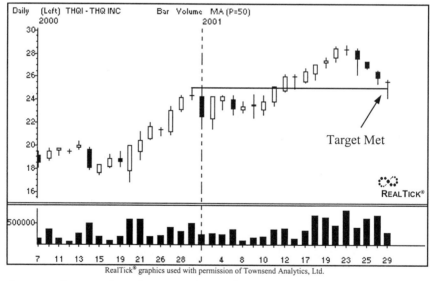

Over the next four trading days, THQI traded down to 24.19 and met the 24.80 target. Although many traders feel uncomfortable shorting stocks that are trending upward, if the reward/risk ratio justifies the trade, professional traders should be encourage to execute it.

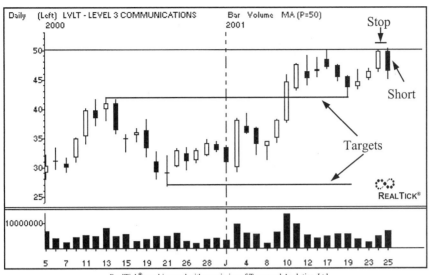

RealTick® graphics used with permission of Townsend Analytics, Ltd.

LVLT showed up on the Sky Scraper Scan when it was trading at 49.20. The stock found resistance at 50.25 for the second time in two days and the third time in seven days. The pattern could end up as a double top pattern. The way to trade this setup is to short the stock at 49.20 and place a stop loss at 50.45 (0.20 over the high of the day). The first price target is the previous tops that were tested successfully around 42 (middle horizontal line). The second price target, should that price level not hold, would be the lows around 27. This would complete the double top pattern. Let's see what happened next.

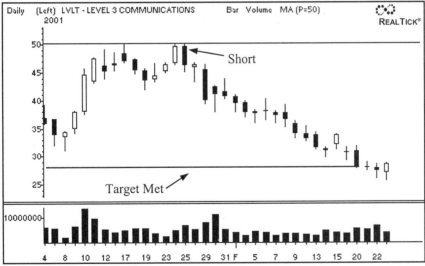

RealTick® graphics used with permission of Townsend Analytics, Ltd.

LVLT trades down through 42, completes the double top pattern, and hit the 27 price target.

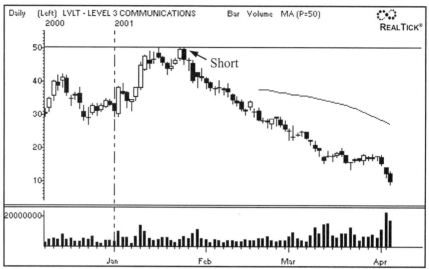

RealTick® graphics used with permission of Townsend Analytics, Ltd.

Following the double top pattern, LVLT trades down 82% before hitting a bottom at 9.13. By using the Sky Scraper Scan, we found LVLT at its pivot point just before it broke down hard. The entry point that day represented very favorable reward/risk ratio.

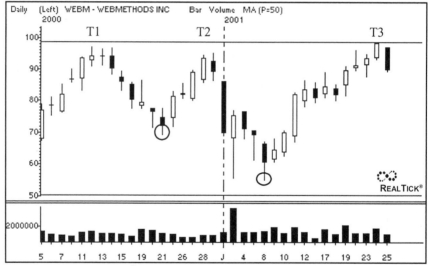

RealTick® graphics used with permission of Townsend Analytics, Ltd.

WEBM showed up on the Sky Scraper Scan when it was trading at 96.50. The stock found resistance at 95-99 for the third time in two months. The pattern could end up as a triple top pattern. The way to trade this setup is to short the stock at 96.50 and place a stop loss at 97.33 (0.20 over the high of the day). The first price target is the previous low at 69 (circle on left). The second price target, should that price level not hold, would be the lows around 55 (circle on right). Let's see what happened next.

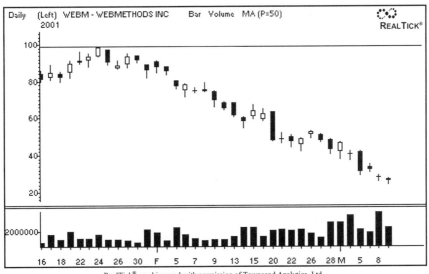

Similar to LVLT, WEBM went down 75% and hit 23. It easily hit both the 69 and 55 price targets. Again, the Sky Scraper Scan found the stock on its pivot day just before it collapsed. This is another example of combining support and resistance levels with the Sky Scraper Scan and executing a high reward/low risk trade. The weakness in the overall market greatly contributed to the sharp decline in both stocks. However, trading these setups based on support and resistance and finding these stocks by using the Sky Scraper Scan proved to be very profitable.

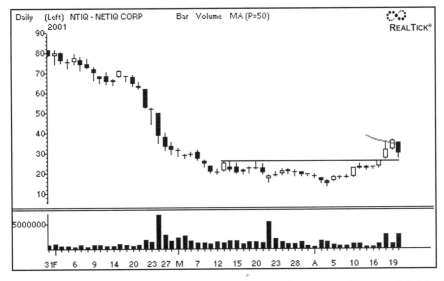

NTIQ showed up on the Sky Scraper Scan when it was trading at 34.50. The stock has enjoyed a nice run from 13.50 in two weeks and found resistance at the 50-day MA. In this case, we short the stock at 34.50 and place a stop loss at 35.30 (0.20 over the high of the day). The price target is 26.20 (horizontal line). Let's see what happens next.

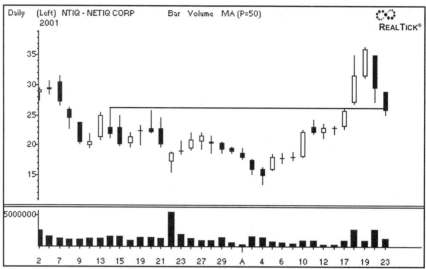

RealTick® graphics used with permission of Townsend Analytics, Ltd.

The following day, NTIQ trades down to 25.17 and hits the 26.20 price target. What I liked about this Sky Scraper setup was that the stock had a big run in a short period time, and it found resistance at the 50-day MA. What I also liked was that the stock was in a longer-term downtrend. This suggested that many investors would take advantage of the rallies to sell their stock at break-even, (this is also known as overhead supply).

The previous four examples show the basics of the Sky Scraper Scan. In the first example, we shorted a strong stock that was making higher highs. In the second example, we shorted a stock that may have formed a double top. In the third example, we shorted a stock that may have formed a triple top. And in the forth example, we shorted a stock that had overhead resistance after it made a big move up and found resistance at the 50-day MA. Although each example is unique, they all have one thing in common - Resistance. The major difference between the setups was the time frame of the resistance, and the pattern itself.

As I said before, the Sky Scraper Scan is a big part of my overall trading system. It allows me to play both sides of the market. There are days in which I will be both long stocks that show up on the Bottom Fisher Scan and short stocks that show up in the Sky Scraper Scan at the same time.

I named this scan Sky Scraper, because it looks for stocks that might have reached the "sky" and formed a short-term top.

CHAPTER **22**

Fundamental Analysis

The magic phrase in Wall Street when it comes to being the proud owner of a stock is Earnings Growth. Every fund manager would love to own shares of a company that is forecasting a bright future in which it will earn more money than it did in the past, forever. In order to find these promising companies, fund managers and investors will engage in fundamental analysis. The process begins by gathering information in the following order:

1. Information about the state of the economy and the economic outlook.
2. Information about particular industries
3. Information about specific companies
4. General information about the stock market

When gathering information about the state of the economy, analysts will look at the different economic indicators available to them. When they try to figure out the economic outlook, however, all they need to do is look at the stock market. According to U.S. Department of Commerce, stock prices are a leading economic indicator. This means that they usually reach peaks and troughs before business cycles change directions. Consequently, analyzing the economic outlook begins with analyzing the price behavior of the stock market. Although I would encourage you to study as much as you possibly can on how to analyze the economy and the meanings of the different economical indicators, I do not think it is a must for stock traders.

When gathering information about particular industries, analysts will consider the economic structure of the industry, supply and demand, industrial life cycle, role of government, and projections of industry trends. One of the key numbers analysts will be looking at is the growth rate of a particular industry, which will be compared to the growth rate of the overall economy as measured by an indicator such as GNP.

When gathering information about a particular company, analysts will examine the company's products, brand names, product life cycle, supply, demand, geographic markets, management team, and financial statements. Again, analysts will be looking at the growth rate of the company, which will be compared to the growth rate of the industry it belongs to.

When studying the financial statements, analysts will study the different ratios and indicators and determine the company's intrinsic value. It all starts with profits, which are the ultimate test of management's effectiveness and are the most important thing to all investors. There are a few ways to measure profits.

Earnings Per Share (EPS)
EPS = Net income / Number of shares outstanding

Return on Equity (ROE)
ROE = Net Income / Common shareholders equity

Return on Assets (ROA)
ROA = Net Income / Total assets

Profit Margin = Net income / Revenues

The reason analysts do all this research is to try and determine if a stock is overvalued or undervalued. Most individuals think of stock values in terms of price per share. They should also think about the market value of a company in terms of market cap, which is the price per share times the number of shares outstanding.

There are a handful of valuation ratios that professionals use such as dividend valuation method, capital asset pricing model, book value, market value exchange ratio, and price to earnings or cash flow ratio.

Price / Earnings Ratio is one of the most widely used methods of determining the value of a stock. This ratio is calculated by dividing the price of a stock by its earnings per share. The problem is that this number is old news! For instance, let's say that Company XYZ has earnings of 10.20 a share and a PE ratio of 4. Company ABCD has earnings of 15 cents a share and a PE ratio of 176. Which one of these companies would you rather buy today?

What we don't know in this example is how much money would these companies make next year. Suppose XYZ is going to make 60 cents next year, and ABCD is also going to make 60 cents next year, which stock would you rather buy today?

XYZ trading at 4 times earnings, 4 X 10.20 = 40.80
ABCD is trading at 176 times earnings = 0.15 X 176 = 26.40

The forward PE ratio, based on the estimates of earnings for next year, are as follows:

XYZ's forward PE ratio = 40.80 / 0.60 = 68

ABCD's forward PE ratio = 26.40 / 0.60 = 44

Based on the above numbers, the decision is easy. ABCD is showing strong earnings growth and is trading at a lower forward PE ratio than XYZ. In general, stocks with low PE ratios are expected to enjoy low growth rate, while stocks with high PE ratios are expected to enjoy high growth rate. The key word is *expected*.

Unfortunately, if something were already expected, then a stock would have made its move in price already. Consequently, fundamental analysis is lagging. Moreover, most of the numbers we can work with as investors are historical numbers, because we do not have access to forward estimates that management has and doesn't normally release until it's too late. Therefore, as stock traders, fundamental analysis is pretty much useless! I strongly believe that if a company has healthy fundamentals it will most likely show up on its price chart, and if it doesn't have strong fundamentals it will most likely also show up on its chart. Thus, spend your time on chart analysis rather than fundamental analysis. If you think I am out of my mind, pay close attention to the next example. The following is an EPS trend and revisions by the analysts covering CSCO.

EPS Trend	This Quarter (7/2001)	Next Quarter (10/2001)	This Year (7/2001)	Next Year (7/2002)
Current	0.03	0.05	0.41	0.29
7 Days Ago	0.02	0.03	0.41	0.29
30 Days Ago	0.08	0.09	0.53	0.56
60 Days Ago	0.14	0.13	0.61	0.71
90 Days Ago	0.20	0.15	0.65	0.81

As you can see, the numbers were changing very fast. Within 83 days, the estimates for next year's earnings went down 64%. This is a substantial downward EPS trend. However, if you bought CSCO at 26 in February expecting earnings of 81 cents a share, you were paying 32 times next year's earnings. That is a very low historical multiple for a stock that was expected at the time to have an average growth of 35% + over the next five years.

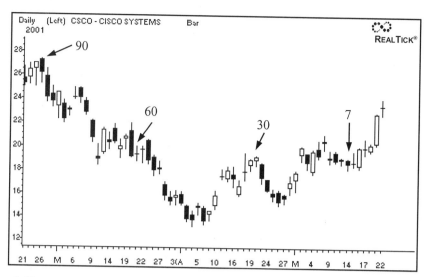

If you followed the chart and used sound money management system, you would have saved a lot of money. What is very interesting though is the fact that the estimates were cut to 56 cents from 71 cents around April 20th and were cut again to 29 cents on May 15th yet, the stock did not trade lower. The PE ratio on the different dates was as follows:

Feb 22nd: PE - 32, March 22nd: PE - 28, April 23rd: PE - 31, May 15th: PE - 64, May 22nd: PE - 80

Although I was able to get my hands on forecasted earnings numbers, even the analysts did not have a clue as to CSCO's future earnings. However, the price chart clued us in as to what was expected to happen way before the analysts made their revisions.

This case study of CSCO magnifies the importance of technical analysis. It shows the changes of investors' expectations prior to the revisions of the estimates. The fundamental data is lagging the obvious conclusions that can be drawn from the chart. A healthy company would have a healthy chart. Let's go back to Feb 22nd, CSCO was not trading at 32 forward PE, it was trading at 90 forward PE. However, there was no way to know that based on the "current" profit estimates published by the analysts. Consequently, you might have thought you were getting a bargain if you used their published numbers as guidelines for your fundamental analysis only to find out that the price of the stock you just bought went down over 50% in the next seven weeks.

As I said earlier in this chapter, I encourage you to study all you can about all the aspects of fundamental analysis and world economy. I just wanted to point out what kind of animal you will be dealing with, and my opinion that the charts are a leading indicator.

Q&A

I hope I answered most of your questions regarding how I trade stocks and what products I use. The following are additional questions taken from the numerous emails I receive on a daily basis. I felt that many of you may have the same questions, so I will answer them in this chapter.

Q: Why are you doing this?
A: On 12/4/97 my son Jordan was born and my life completely changed. As a father, my only wish for him besides good health is for all his dreams to come true. It didn't take me too long to realized that my son will need all the help he can get in order to fulfill his dreams. This reality has been the driving force behind all my work. My philosophy is simple. If I will do all I can to help fulfill the dreams of others, in the future, someone will return the favor to my son.

Q: Do you believe anyone can be a successful trader?
A: As much as I hate to answer a question with a question, I must do so. Can anyone be a brain surgeon, a lawyer, a senator, or even a secretary? More importantly, would everyone be happy to be in anyone of those fields? The answer is no. If I was to answer the question in a political way, I would say that anyone with qualities a, b, c, d, e, and t, can be successful at it, but that is not how you asked the question.

Q: What does it take to be successful in this business?
A: Mastering every word in this book and having the discipline to apply it on a daily basis.

Q: Do you get paid a referral fee if I open an account with a broker?
A: Absolutely not!

Q: Do you get paid commissions on my trades if I open an account with a broker?
A: Absolutely not!

Q: Do you get paid if I order a computer from TriKinetic?
A: Absolutely not!

Q: Do you get paid a referral fee if I use RealTick?
A: Absolutely not!

Q: Which broker do you recommend?
A: I recommend that you have an account with a broker that you can trust. I

suggest you interview your broker and know all his strength and weaknesses before you execute the first trade.

Q: Do you manage other people's money?
A: No, I don't.

Q: Are you going to manage other people's money?
A: Honesty, I had many offers to manage multi-million dollar accounts in the past, and I have declined them all. At this point of my life, I enjoy all the freedom in my work.

Q: Should I read your other books?
A: This is a tough question. Since I can't be objective, I will say that you need to ask someone else who has read them.

Q: Should I read any other books?
A: Absolutely! However, you must take time between readings. You need to absorb what you have read and try to see if you can incorporate it into your trading system, before you can move on to the next book. Patience is a must!

Q: Should I mention your name once getting a product you recommended?
A: There is no financial gain for me, but it might help the company you are doing business with track their referrals or marketing efforts. If you do mention my name and receive bad service, please let me know as soon as possible.

Q: How can I get the Tony Oz Calculator?
A: You will need to go to *www.tonyoz.com* and download it. If you are asked for downloading password or code, please enter the word *happy*.

Q: How can I get a hold of you?
A: You can find my contact information if you click the *contact us* link on the *www.tonyoz.com* website

Q: Is there anything else important that you want to tell us?
A: Yes, Have Fun and Trade Smart!

The Tony Oz Training Program

This training program is designed to help you create your own personalized trading system. While many might argue that the basics can be learned in a few weeks, I truly believe that it takes time and hard work to progress and achieve a solid foundation. As I showed you in this book, my personal trading system is the fruit of fifteen years in the stock market.

The most common error that exists in the expectations of individuals is closely related to the misconception that the stock market is a *get rich quick* scheme. On the contrary, the stock market is more of a *go broke in a week* scheme than a *get rich quick* scheme. Those who want to make a million in a day will be hung in a week. Consequently, the program I designed will require time, patience, and hard work.

The goal of this program is to help you develop a trading system that is tailored to your own personality. I recommend that you have a complete understanding of every chapter in this book prior to proceeding with this program. If you had any difficulty understanding some of the chapters, you must read them again. If you think you are ready to begin this program, then proceed. For best results, I recommend that you do not place any trades during the duration of this training program.

I understand that the experience of the readers of this book varies all the way from true beginners to hedge fund managers. Consequently, I created three different programs to accommodate that. The beginner program takes eight weeks to complete. The beginner/intermediate program takes six weeks to complete, and the intermediate/advanced program takes four weeks to complete.

You will need to download the calculator and use RealTick®. Although I can't promise anything, I will do my best to arrange for a special deal with quote providers for the duration of this training program, so please check the website for any special offers. Once you have RealTick® up and running, you can start the training program.

Once you are ready to start the training program, you will need to register online at *www.tonyoz.com* or email us a request for the training program. Once your request is processed, you will receive precise instructions on how to proceed. While you are taking the training program, you will need to download and install custom RealTick® pages that I designed especially for this program. Consequently, we will need to know how many monitors you have. All pages for single or dual monitors are at 1024 X 768 res. If you are running higher resolution, you may need to resize some of the windows.